Best Recipes of Berkshire Chefs

Best Recipes of

Berkshire Chefs

MIRIAM JACOBS

Foreword by
Ruth Adams Bronz

Berkshire House Publishers
Stockbridge, Massachusetts

BEST RECIPES OF BERKSHIRE CHEFS
© 1993 by Berkshire House Publishers

Library of Congress Cataloging-in-Publication Data
Jacobs, Miriam
Best recipes of Berkshire chefs / by Miriam Jacobs.
p. cm.
Includes index.
ISBN 0-936399-35-X : $12.95
1. Cookery, American. 2. Cookery—Massachusetts—Berkshire County.
I. Title.
TX715.J218 1993
641.5'09744'1—dc20   93-16932
CIP

FEATURED ON THE FRONT COVER:

Chocolate Caramel Pie from 20 Railroad Street;
Shrimp Salad with Citrus Sections & Celery Poppy Dressing from The Red Lion Inn;
Homard Bouillabaisse from La Tomate Bistro; *Apple Juice-Sweetened Muffins* and *Chocolate Chip Cookies* from The Berkshire Coffee Roasting Company;
Chilled Asparagus in Sesame Sauce from The Castle Street Café.
Vegetables, fruit, and flowers from Taft Farms.

Editor and Designer: Rodelinde Albrecht
Illustration: Elizabeth Barbour
Cover Design: Christine Swirnoff
Cover Photograph: © Dan McCoy/Rainbow
Managing Editor: Sarah Novak
Production Services: Quality Printing and Ripinsky & Co.

Berkshire House books are available at substantial discounts for bulk purchases by corporations and other organizations for promotions and premiums. Special personalized editions can also be produced in large quantities.
For more information, contact:
Berkshire House Publishers
Box 297, Stockbridge MA 01262
800-321-8526

Manufactured in the United States of America
First printing 1993
10 9 8 7 6 5 4 3 2 1

For my Mom
Selma Jacobs van Praagh
who fed me her good cooking
and nourished me with her love

Contents

BRUNCH & LUNCH

ENTRÉES

SIDE DISHES

VEGETABLES & SALADS

Sample Menus

SUMMER LUNCH

Cold Blueberry Soup 31

Herb Yellowfin Tuna with Warm Pepper Salad 42

Lime Cheesecake 145

BUFFET FOR A COCKTAIL PARTY

Rilette 3

Caponata 18

Polenta Timbales with Spicy Eggplant Sauce 84

Honey Mustard Shrimp 121

Veal & Shiitake Roulades with Port Wine Glaze 56

Samara's Sesame Noodle Sauce 92

Baked Mushroom Loaf 123

Flourless Chocolate Mousse Cake 133

Swedish Hallon Rutor 128

& French bread from a local bakery

DOWN-HOME SUPPER

Beef & Vegetable Stew 54

Popovers 48

Embree's Mashed Potatoes 98

Perfect Corn on the Cob 106

Grandma Horka's Plum Cake 143

BIG LAWN PICNIC

Gazpacho 29

Peasant Bread Appetizer with Whole Roasted Garlic 10

Chilled Asparagus in Sesame Sauce 115

Shrimp Salad with Citrus Sections & Celery Poppy Dressing 111

Lemon Pie 152

BERKSHIRE WINTER BRUNCH

Smoked Salmon 4

Farmers' Market Apple French Toast 37

Lemon Yogurt Cake 140

Hot Mulled Cider 49

& fresh bagels from a local bakery

LUNCH ON THE APPALACHIAN TRAIL

Creamy Lowfat Hummus 16

Panzanella 124

Apricot Almond Granola Bars 127

Apple Herbal 130

& pita wedges

AFTER-THEATER SNACK

Alice's Special Shrimp 75
Chocolate Caramel Pie 146

WINTER HOLIDAY MEAL

Fried Parmesan Mushrooms with Shallot Vinaigrette 12
Butternut Squash & Cider Soup 26
Herb-Infused Baby Pheasant au Jus 66
Baked Artichokes with Onions & Sweet Peppers 104
Sautéed Red Cabbage with Walnuts and Chèvre 103
Green Salad with Raspberry Vinaigrette 116
Apple Cranberry Pie 150
Pumpkin Chocolate Cheesecake 144

SUMMER GRILL

Grilled Leeks with Bacon Vinaigrette 6
Strawberry Lemon Soup 30
Chicken Satay 120
Grilled Tofu Kebabs 122
Hot Blueberries with Vanilla Ice Cream 158

AFTER-SKATING PARTY

Spanish Soup 23
White Bean Chili with Grilled Chicken 41
Butterscotch Schnapps Pie 147

Best Recipes: The Sources

Bartlett's Orchard
Swamp Road, Richmond
413-698-2559

The Berkshire Coffee
  Roasting Company
286 Main Street
Great Barrington
413-528-5505

Berkshire Place Gourmet
  Foods
Main Street, Egremont
413-528-5620

Blantyre
Route 20, Lenox
413-637-3356

Boiler Room Café
405 Stockbridge Road
Great Barrington
413-528-4280

Canyon Ranch
  in the Berkshires
91 Kemble Street, Lenox
413-637-4100

Castle Street Café
10 Castle Street
Great Barrington
413-528-5244

Chez Vous Caterers
Stockbridge
413-298-4278

Church Street Café
69 Church Street, Lenox
413-637-2745

Cobble Café
27 Spring Street
Williamstown
413-458-5930

Cranwell Resort & Hotel
55 Lee Road, Lenox
413-637-1364

Dos Amigos
  Mexican Restaurant
250 Stockbridge Road
Great Barrington
413-528-0084

Dragon Breads
Stockbridge
413-298-5204

The Egremont Inn
Old Sheffield Road
South Egremont
413-528-2111

Elizabeth's Restaurant
1264 East Street, Pittsfield
413-448-8244

The Elm Court Inn
Plain Road, North Egremont
413-528-0325

Embree's Restaurant
Main Street, Housatonic
413-274-3476

Encore! Encore!
Berkshire Hilton Inn
Berkshire Common
Pittsfield
413-499-2000

Hancock Shaker Village
Routes 41 and 20, Pittsfield
413-443-0188

Joe's Diner
63 Center Street, Lee
413-243-9756

John Andrew's Restaurant
Route 23, South Egremont
413-528-3469

La Tomate Bistro
293 Main Street
Great Barrington
413-528-3003

Martin's Restaurant
49 Railroad Street
Great Barrington
413-528-5455

Naomi's Herbs
11 Housatonic Street
Lenox
413-637-0616

The Old Inn on the Green
Route 57
New Marlborough
413-229-3131

Rawson Brook Farm
New Marlborough Road
Monterey
413-528-2138

The Red Lion Inn
Main Street, Stockbridge
413-298-5545

The Roseborough Grill
83 Church Street, Lenox
413-637-2700

Sadie's Pies
Route 41
West Stockbridge
413-232-4382

Seekonk Pines Inn
142 Seekonk Cross Road
Great Barrington
413-528-4192

The Springs Restaurant
Route 7, New Ashford
413-458-3465

Suchèle Bakers
31 Housatonic Street
Lenox
413-637-0939

Taft Farms
Route 183
Great Barrington
413-528-1515

Truffles & Such
Allendale
  Shopping Center
Pittsfield
413-442-0151

20 Railroad Street
Great Barrington
413-528-9345

The Weathervane Inn
Route 23, South Egremont
413-528-9580

The Williamsville Inn
Route 41, West Stockbridge
413-274-6118

Windflower Inn
Route 23, Great Barrington
413-528-2720

The Wright Pasta Company
Route 23, South Egremont
413- 528-6930

Foreword

When I moved to the Berkshires, I had lived in New York for eight years, a refugee from Texas. I'm still a New Yorker, though I've lived part and full time in Massachusetts for twenty years. I have a house in Housatonic, a block from the river; I ran a restaurant in West Stockbridge for four years in the seventies and early eighties.

And though I've never loved any place as much, I don't feel entirely at home here, and it took me ten of my twenty years in the Berkshires to figure out why. Coming out of my house on a late summer afternoon, I looked over Monument Mountain at a perfect dark-blue sky, with a perfect Persian sliver of a moon hanging in it, and a perfect evening star seeming to depend from the bottom tip of its crescent. It was as if I'd never been there before—it was as beautiful as if I'd just driven up from New York for the first time and seen the blue haze on the hills, the intensity of the sky's color, the clarity of the air. And that was it: it's too beautiful a place ever to get used to, to take for granted as we think of taking home for granted; the eye is always surprised, the spirit taken off guard.

So I started cooking seriously in the best of all physical settings, at a time when most of the best cooking in the Berkshires was being done at home—other than the Red Lion Inn and Joe's Diner, there were precious few places to eat out in 1972. Before I cooked for my own restaurant, I had five years of long-weekend cooking in the Berkshires—Randy Wagner stuffed pumpkins, Kate de Garamo roasted venison, and Joan and David Loveless and twenty-five or so of us pit-roasted lamb on more than one Fourth of July.

It was one long feast, and it taught me that seasonality is the secret of most good cooking—we talked about the corn and tomatoes before they came in each summer; we thought about strawberries and raspberries when it was still too cold to go to the Green River to swim; we bought great Italian sausage and kielbasa at Ptak's and made a game of thinking of new ways to cook them.

Well, a lot of us still think of what to cook next as the day's foremost topic, but we're no longer limited to our own kitchens or those we visit—the restaurant has come to the Berkshires in a serious way. The Red Lion is still dispensing superior inn food and civilized cocktails, and it's been joined by more good places to eat out than I ever supposed would settle here—La Tomate for lovely Provençal food; Clayton Hambrick's eclectic, satisfying menu at the Church Street Café; Embree's, which gives us that best of tomato salads, panzanella, all summer; Martin's for pancakes; the Coffee Roasting Company for, thank heaven and at last, cappuccino. . . . The list goes on and on, so that we're tempted out of our own kitchens a lot more often than would have seemed possible a scant ten years ago.

And the Berkshires are still the best place in the world to cook—the seasons are so distinct that they positively tell you what to do: "Make that butternut squash soup in October!" "It's definitely time for summer pudding in July." "It's August and you haven't done anything with corn in at least two days!" "Quit complaining about that glut of zucchini and mix it with the tomatoes—you'll love them." It's a serious running subtext that goes on all the time, giving the year and our cooking a definite shape and substance.

In my cooking career I've discovered how various the food of America is, and how welcoming and interesting the palates of Berkshire County are. Miriam has obviously had a wonderful time with this book—and how fortunate we are to have it. Enjoy the pleasures of Berkshire cooking!

Ruth Adams Bronz
New York City

Preface

The Berkshires have always attracted an interesting melange of people, visitors and residents alike, past and present: literary greats Herman Melville, Nathaniel Hawthorne, and Edith Wharton; artists Norman Rockwell and Daniel Chester French; the austere Shakers and wealthy "Gilded Age" socialites.

And no wonder. The setting of natural beauty is enticing year-round: hills and woods for hiking and skiing, lakes for swimming and skating. The county's pretty towns and their welcoming inns look like subjects for a Norman Rockwell painting—and probably were. And these days the Boston Symphony Orchestra summers at Tanglewood, Jacob's Pillow hosts the nation's oldest summer dance festival, theater productions from Shakespeare to modern drama are presented throughout the county, and there are museums, galleries, and historic homes.

Not surprisingly, the range of culinary experiences to be found in the Berkshires mirrors the interesting variety of its people and landscape. Whether you want the perfect plain meatloaf sandwich or nothing short of a four-star, five-course meal with wines from three continents, you'll find it here.

At Berkshire lunch counters, good cooks serve up real food: their own famous pancakes, stews, or chili. At inns and restaurants here, chefs take pride in using locally grown produce and other local products to fashion new and inspired meals. Local shiitakes, tomatoes, apples, milk, corn, pasta, bread, and chèvre, to mention a few things, all find their way onto Berkshire dining room tables in various guises. On the other hand, Berkshire chefs will also wow you with ingredients from all over the country and the world.

With all this inspiration, Berkshire home cooks also work magic. Even bake sale items here are legendary: people look forward all year to getting a Chocolate Almond Cake at the Berkshire Country Day School Spring Fair!

One of my favorite things to do in the Berkshires is to organize a picnic to enjoy on the grounds before an outdoor performance at Tanglewood, or at The Mount for Shakespeare & Co. Then I like to walk around before the performance to see what other picnics are offering, and steal an idea or two from them. It's part of the performance.

I came to the Berkshires the long way around: a Dutch native, born in Uruguay, some years in India, and then in New York. I have called the Berkshires home for nearly a decade now. Whether you come here for a visit or for a lifetime, enjoy this very special corner of the world. And enjoy the recipes in this book. As they say where I come from, "eet smakelijk!"

Acknowledgments

A book is never a solitary project. My thanks goes out to all the chefs in the Berkshires who so generously contributed their recipes and who had the patience to answer my questions.

The idea for the book was created by David Emblidge, and he was the one who signed me on. He is responsible for my writing in the cooking field; without his help I might have never have had the courage to start my first cooking column. I also want to thank him for the hours of computer advice, writing lessons, and editorial help, all seasoned by his good judgment and longstanding experience in the publishing and writing field, and all offered with generous measures of humor and patience.

I would like to thank Sarah Novak, managing editor, for her willingness to make this seem easy.

Thanks to Rodelinde Albrecht for editing, designing, and typesetting, and doing all of it so very well: her meticulous work and well-thought-out and intelligent decisions were an inspiration.

Thanks to Betty Barbour for her wonderful illustrations.

Thanks also to Peggy Rousseau, Jean Rousseau, Michael Gladishev, Sarah Novak, and especially Mary Osak, for their assistance in compiling information about the restaurants and food purveyors.

I want to thank my kids Sarah, Abigail, and Adam for keeping the faith and for encouraging my efforts even when that meant eating weird stuff.

Thank you, David, for your love.

Thanks, Dad, for teaching me about being organized and loving hard work and about doing the right thing just because. And thanks for all the love.

Thanks, Mom, for the countless meals, the good health we enjoyed in large part because of your efforts, for always believing in me, and for your endless supply of love.

Miriam Jacobs
Stockbridge

APPETIZERS

Rilette

LA TOMATE

*Rilette is a traditional French dish. In America, legendary cookbook author
James Beard has observed, this dish is often served in French restaurants.
Jean Claude Vierne, chef of La Tomate, says that
"this version is the one that an expatriate Frenchman will say is 'just like home'."*

Preheat the oven to 400°.

Sauté the pork, diced bacon, and onion until the onion is transparent. Add the sage, salt and pepper to taste, cayenne pepper, water, thyme, and bay leaves.

Place the mixture into an ovenproof pan and cook at 400° for 1-1/2 hour. Reduce the oven temperature to 275° and cook for another 30 minutes.

Remove from the oven and discard the bay leaves, thyme, and pork bones. Coarsely grind the whole preparation in a food processor.

Place into a large terrine and chill. Garnish with cornichons and serve with garlic croutons or French bread.

SERVES 8

2 pounds pork butt
   and bone
2 cups diced slab bacon
1 cup chopped onion
1 cup chopped fresh
   sage
Salt and pepper
Pinch of cayenne
   pepper
2 cups water
2 sprigs of fresh thyme
2 large bay leaves
Cornichons (French
   gherkins) for garnish
Garlic croutons (see
   page 73) or French
   bread slices

Smoked Salmon

YEHUDA HANANI

*Yehuda Hanani is a distinguished cellist who has performed with major orchestras
of the world, in recitals, and on award-winning recordings. He is currently artistic
director of the "Close Encounters with Music" series at The Berkshire Museum.
"This recipe came originally from our friend Albert Langman in Malibu.
We have found the results of this preparation to be superior to any
of the commercially available smoked salmon—surpassing it in tenderness
and delicacy. In fact, knowing we could cut the umbilical cord from some of our favorite
New York delis made the move to the Berkshires that much less traumatic!
Composers have shown a particular enthusiasm for this recipe. Aaron Copland asked
for thirds at a dinner party in our apartment. In Aspen, as we discussed
the concerto composer Bernard Rands was writing for me, rounds of aquavit
were punctuated with robust helpings of this salmon. The concerto is called 'Hiraeth,'
which means longing for home, and we imagine that the salmon
was very much a staple of Bernard's boyhood Wales."*

YIELDS 2 to 2-1/2 pounds

Salmon fillet,
   preferably North
   Atlantic (choose a
   meaty piece, not too
   close to the tail)
3 tablespoons kosher
   salt
1 tablespoon sugar
1 to 1-1/2 tablespoon
   liquid smoke
   flavoring (Wright's
   Liquid Smoke is
   recommended)

Cut the salmon fillet lengthwise into two equal pieces. Wipe the scales, but do not wash the salmon. Using a knife, pull out any remaining bones against the grain.

Mix the salt and sugar on a piece of wax paper. Dampen with the liquid smoke flavoring and then mix well again.

Coat the fillets uniformly with the smoke mixture, brushing the top and sides. Stack the two fillets, matching the thick sides to the thin sides, with the skin sides to the exterior of the fillet sandwich. Use the wax paper to slip the whole into a plastic zipper storage bag. (Do not leave the wax paper in the bag.) Pour any remaining liquid smoke mixture over the top.

Zip the bag shut, pushing out all the air. Refrigerate for 5 or 6 days, turning over every 24 hours.

Open the bag and let all the juices run out. Line a platter with paper towels and place on it half of the fish, meat side up. Place another paper towel on the top and press down lightly to remove all the free liquid from the top, bottom, and sides. Then drizzle oil over the fish and rub it in well with a paper towel on the top and sides to minimize dehydration. Repeat with the other half of the fish. Slice as thinly as possible using a very sharp knife.

Serve with Bermuda onion, capers, and pumpernickel or rye.

Freezes extremely well for up to seven weeks. To serve, let the salmon sit at room temperature until thawed, and then slice.

Mild-flavored oil

Accompaniments:
Sliced Bermuda onion
Capers
Hearty pumpernickel
  or rye

Grilled Leeks with Bacon Vinaigrette

THE ELM COURT INN

*The Elm Court Inn is a country guest house and restaurant in North Egremont.
Chef Urs Bieri came to the Elm Court from his former position as chef
at the United Nations, and calls his style of cooking "innovative Continental."
He offers a range of health-conscious entrées—and a dessert menu
renowned for its luscious creations.*

SERVES 4

4 medium leeks
2 quarts water
Pinch of salt
6 slices of bacon
1/2 bunch of parsley,
   minced
1/2 bunch of chives,
   minced
3 tablespoons minced
   onion
1/2 cup olive oil
1 tablespoon mustard
4 tablespoons balsamic
   vinegar
Salt and pepper

Cut the leeks in half lengthwise, but do not remove the roots, or the leeks will fall apart. Rinse them very well under running water to get out all the sand. Bring the water and salt to a boil in a large stock pot. Carefully place the leeks into the boiling water; cover and boil for 5 to 6 minutes. Remove the leeks and chill them quickly in ice water. Set the leeks aside to drain.

Cook the bacon until crisp; remove from the pan and let cool, reserving the rendered fat.

In a mixing bowl, combine the parsley, chives, onion, oil, mustard, and balsamic vinegar. Add the bacon fat and two of the bacon slices, chopped. This vinaigrette will improve in flavor if prepared a day in advance. Season to taste with salt and pepper.

You can now grill the leeks on the barbecue or under a broiler. Dry the cooled leeks, brush them with oil, and place on the grill with the cut side away from the heat source. Turn over and cook the other side. (Total grilling time is approximately 8 to 10 minutes.)

To serve, place the leeks on a platter and pour the vinaigrette on top. Garnish with tomatoes and eggs if desired, and the remaining four bacon slices.

Oil for brushing on
    the leeks
Chopped tomatoes for
    garnish
Sliced hardboiled eggs
    for garnish

Zucchini, Wild Rice & Sun-Dried Tomato Pancakes with Wild Mushrooms

TRUFFLES & SUCH

Award-winning chef Irene Maston has worked a miracle. She creates delicious, imaginative, and wholesome dishes that please every palate— all in Pittsfield's Allendale Shopping Center. Maston is recognized in Massachusetts as one of its leading seafood chefs—a considerable honor, given the Berkshires' location! But her talent does not stop there. Chef Irene's creativity with vegetables, greens, and cheeses make all the menu choices as beautiful in their presentation as they are delicious to eat.

SERVES 8

Wild mushrooms:

1/2 ounce dried cèpes or porcini
1 cup water
2 tablespoons olive oil
2 tablespoons minced shallot
1-1/2 teaspoon minced garlic
8 ounces fresh shiitake mushrooms, sliced
1/4 cup brandy
1/2 cup vermouth
1 tablespoon hoisin sauce
1 cup heavy cream

To prepare the wild mushrooms:
Reconstitute the dried cèpes in the water. Drain, reserving the water, and dice the mushrooms.

In a frying pan, slowly sauté in the olive oil the shallot, garlic, and shiitake mushrooms until softened. Deglaze the pan with the brandy and vermouth.

Add the hoisin sauce, diced cèpes, and reserved liquid. Simmer until the liquid is reduced by half.

Add the heavy cream and bring to a boil; reduce the heat and simmer until thickened.

To make the pancakes:
Combine all the ingredients until just mixed. Let the batter rest for 30 minutes.

In a 12-inch pan, heat 1/4 cup olive oil. Drop the batter into the oil by quarter-cupfuls and cook each side until golden brown.

Serve the pancakes with the wild mushroom sauce, garnished with sun-dried tomatoes.

Pancakes:
1 cup shredded
  zucchini
1/2 cup cooked wild
  rice
2 eggs
1/3 cup flour
1/4 cup milk
1/4 cup sun-dried
  tomatoes
1/2 teaspoon minced
  garlic
1/4 teaspoon black
  pepper

1/4 cup olive oil
  for frying
Sliced sun-dried
  tomatoes for garnish

Peasant Bread Appetizer
with Whole Roasted Garlic

JOHN ANDREW'S RESTAURANT

Chef Dan Smith recommends firm garlic with tight skins for best results. Also, if you like, you can use kalamata or niçoise olives. Don't be intimidated by the large quantity of garlic: once it is roasted, its flavor is mild and sweet.

SERVES 6

6 firm heads of garlic
2 tablespoons unsalted butter
2 pinches of salt
Freshly ground pepper
3/4 cup olive oil
3/4 cup sun-dried tomatoes
1/2 cup oil-cured black olives
3/4 cup goat cheese
3/4 cup cream cheese

Preheat the oven to 275°.

Peel the outer skin off the garlic heads, leaving one layer of skin around the outer cloves so that the head of garlic remains intact. Place the heads into a baking pan just large enough to hold them. Dot with the butter and sprinkle with a pinch of salt and pepper.

Cover the baking pan with foil and roast at 275° for 2-1/4 to 2-1/2 hours, depending on the size of the garlic heads. Baste with olive oil after the first hour and again after 30 minutes. The garlic is done when it is soft and creamy like warm butter.

While the garlic is roasting, soak the sun-dried tomatoes in water until softened, then dry and chop them.

Remove the pits from the olives and chop.

With an electric mixer, combine the goat cheese and cream cheese until smooth.

Just before serving, toast the peasant bread, spread with the creamed cheeses, and top with the chopped tomatoes and olives. On warmed plates, arrange the roasted garlic and slices of peasant bread, and drizzle with the olive oil used in roasting the garlic. Now squeeze the garlic onto the bread and eat.

1 loaf of peasant bread, cut into 12 thick slices

Fried Parmesan Mushrooms
with Shallot Vinaigrette

THE BOILER ROOM CAFÉ

No, the Boiler Room Café is not in a boiler room—although it used to be. Instead, it's in a charming house just north of Great Barrington's downtown. The atmosphere inside is both warm and stylish, with exotic flower arrangements and contemporary sculpture against deep red walls. Owner Michèle Miller likes to greet guests at the door, and takes pride in the café's seamless service, both gracious and competent. The cuisine is a combination of American and Continental country—simultaneously hearty and sophisticated.

SERVES 6 to 8

1 pound mushrooms
1 cup flour
1 egg
1 teaspoon water
1/2 cup freshly grated
   Parmesan

Shallot vinaigrette:
2 tablespoons white
   or red wine vinegar
6 tablespoons
   extra-virgin olive oil
1/2 teaspoon herb salt
1 large shallot, minced
2 teaspoons capers
Freshly ground pepper

Clean the mushrooms carefully with a damp cloth. Dip them in the flour, tapping lightly to shake off any excess.

In a bowl, beat together the egg and water. One at a time, drop the mushrooms into the egg and turn them carefully with a fork to draw the egg mixture totally around the flour. Do this very quickly or the egg coating will fall apart.

Roll each mushroom in the Parmesan to coat. Place the prepared mushrooms onto a rack to dry.

To make the shallot vinaigrette:
Mix together well the vinegar, olive oil, herb salt, shallot, capers, and pepper to taste.

BEST RECIPES OF BERKSHIRE CHEFS

To fry the mushrooms:
Pour 1 inch of oil into a large skillet. Over a high flame heat the oil to 350°. You can test for readiness by dropping a cube of bread into the hot oil. It should immediately bubble up and brown.

A few at a time, drop the prepared mushrooms into the oil and fry them until brown on one side. Turn and fry on the other side until the color is uniform. Remove the mushrooms from the hot oil with tongs and drain on paper towels.

Serve immediately, topped with shallot vinaigrette and a generous sprinkling of chopped parsley.

Oil for frying
Chopped parsley
for garnish

Corn & Red Onion Fritters
with Pimiento Jalapeño Sauce

RUTH BRONZ

*These fritters were a popular item at Miss Ruby's Café, the legendary
West Stockbridge eatery of the late '70s. Ruth Bronz, "Miss Ruby" herself,
credits Charlie Kahlstrom, the restaurant's sous chef, with the recipe's creation.
Ruth has enjoyed a cooking and writing career in Texas, New York, and the Berkshires,
and is the author of* Miss Ruby's American Cooking *and* Miss Ruby's Cornucopia,
published by HarperCollins, and of the forthcoming The Third Coast: American Gulf
Coast Cooking, *published by Stewart, Tabori & Chang. Ruth is currently
working on a television series about American regional cooking,
and has plans for a new Berkshire restaurant.*

MAKES *2 dozen fritters
and 8 cups of sauce*

Fritters:
2 cups all-purpose flour
1 cup pastry flour
2 tablespoons baking
   powder
1 teaspoon salt
2 eggs
2 cups diced red onion
3 cups corn kernels and
   their milk fresh off
   the ear, or 3 cups
   canned corn with its
   juice
1-1/2 cup milk,
   approximately
1-1/2 quart soy oil
   for frying

To make the fritters:
Sift together the flours, baking powder,
and salt. Stir in the remaining ingredients except the milk and oil and then
moisten with just enough milk to produce a dropping batter.

Heat the oil to 375°, and drop in fritters
by the generous teaspoonful. Fry until
golden brown, about 5 minutes.

BEST RECIPES OF BERKSHIRE CHEFS

To make the pimiento jalapeño sauce:

In a 2-quart saucepan, melt the butter and stir in the flour. Cook while stirring for 10 minutes without browning.

Meanwhile, scald the milk.

Add the milk to the butter-and-flour mixture all at once, whisking constantly until the sauce is completely smooth.

Add the cheddar cheese and stir until melted. Stir in the pimientos and jalapeños. Add salt to taste.

Pimiento jalapeño sauce:

1/2 cup unsalted butter
3/4 cup flour
6 cups milk
4 ounces sharp cheddar cheese, grated
2 cups chopped pimientos and their juice
1-1/2 cup chopped jalapeños en escabeche (pickled) and their juice
Salt

Creamy Lowfat Hummus

ELEANOR TILLINGHAST

"This hummus is deliciously different. Discarding the oil from the sesame tahini (generally about 3/8 cup) saves some 720 fat calories, but doesn't sacrifice flavor; this is an irresistibly creamy, rich-tasting hummus. As a bonus, the proportions are simple to remember." A former political media consultant, Eleanor Tillinghast moved to the Berkshires in the mid-eighties and started a mail-order business selling gourmet health foods. She is now writing a series of international lowfat cookbooks and a comprehensive guide to healthful cooking.

SERVES 4 to 8

1 heaping tablespoon
   sesame tahini
1 can (15 ounces)
   garbanzo beans
1 medium lemon
1 medium clove of
   garlic
Salt if needed

At the store, select a jar of sesame tahini in which the oil has clearly separated. (Arrowhead Mills brand is organic, separates well, and lacks the unpleasant bitterness of some other brands.)

At home, open the jar of sesame tahini; drain off and discard the oil.

Drain the garbanzo beans, reserving the liquid. (American Prairie Organic brand is a good choice.)

Crush the garlic with a mortar and pestle or a garlic press (mincing will yield less flavor).

Submerge the uncut lemon in very hot water for 2 minutes to release more juice. Juice the lemon.

In a food processor (an electric blender will take longer), blend the garbanzos, the tahini, three quarters of the lemon juice, and the crushed garlic until smooth and creamy.

With the processor or blender running slowly, add the reserved liquid from the garbanzos until the hummus has the desired creaminess.

Taste and adjust flavors, adding more lemon juice and sesame tahini if necessary. You may wish to add a little salt to taste.

This recipe can easily be multiplied.

Caponata

WINDFLOWER INN

*Though this Sicilian dish is featured here as an appetizer,
it can also be served as a relish or salad. This is perfect with French bread,
and highly recommended as picnic fare.*

SERVES 10 to 12

1/3 cup olive oil
3 cups cubed eggplant
1/3 cup diced green
   bell pepper
1 medium onion,
   chopped
4-ounce can mushroom
   stems and pieces
2 cloves garlic, minced
3 tablespoons capers
1/4 cup white wine
6-ounce can tomato
   paste
8-ounce can tomato
   sauce
10-ounce jar salad
   olives
2 tablespoons red wine
   vinegar

In a large skillet, heat the olive oil and add the eggplant, green pepper, onion, mushrooms, and garlic. Cover the skillet and simmer for 10 minutes, stirring occasionally.

Add the remaining ingredients and simmer, covered, for about 30 minutes. If the mixture seems too liquid at the end of the cooking period, uncover for the last few minutes to reduce the liquid.

Cool and refrigerate. Keeps quite well for one week.

Fish à la Russe

MICHAEL GLADISHEV

*"This is my mother's recipe for my favorite dish, a traditional Russian 'zakuska,'
or cold appetizer. The dish can also be served warm as a main course with boiled
new potatoes or as the centerpiece of a picnic." During his non-kitchen hours,
Michael is the Sales and Marketing Director of Berkshire House Publishers.*

Preheat the oven to 350°.

Cut the fish into serving pieces, wash them, and pat them dry. Salt and pepper them to taste. Place the flour into a bowl and roll the fish pieces in the flour to coat.

Pour some oil into a skillet and lightly fry the fish pieces over moderate heat. Transfer the fried fish pieces to a baking dish and set aside.

In the same skillet, sauté the vegetables, adding a bit of oil if necessary. When the vegetables are soft, add the rest of the ingredients, except the parsley and dill. Bring the mixture to a boil and pour over the fish.

Cover the baking dish with aluminum foil and bake at 350° for 20 minutes.

Remove the dish from the oven and sprinkle with the chopped parsley and dill. Refrigerate for several hours or overnight, and serve chilled or at room temperature.

SERVES 4

1-1/2 pound firm fish, such as cod, haddock, or flounder
Salt and pepper
Flour
Oil
1 medium onion, thinly sliced
1/2 green bell pepper, chopped or sliced
2 cloves of garlic, chopped
1 stalk of celery, chopped
1 carrot, shredded
1 teaspoon paprika
2 teaspoons ketchup
1 cup cold water
1/2 teaspoon sugar
1 envelope chicken broth
Chopped fresh parsley and dill for garnish

APPETIZERS

19

SOUPS

Spanish Soup

ROY BLOUNT, JR.

Roy offers assurance that his method of making this soup, though admittedly imprecise, has always worked for him. Roy Blount, Jr., a part-time resident of the Berkshires, is the author of Camels Are Easy, Comedy Is Hard, *and a writer of food poems.*

"It's nice if the beans are dried ones soaked overnight and the tomatoes and greens are fresh (unless the tomatoes are old, hard, pale supermarket ones). But if the beans are canned and the tomatoes are canned (whole) and the greens are frozen, it's all right too.

"Since this soup is Spanish, chorizo sausage is best, but other kinds will do.

"Assemble the vegetable ingredients in a pot at a ratio that seems about right to you, and bring them up to approximately a boil.

"Slice the sausage into sections and sauté them a bit in a skillet to get rid of some of the fat and bring out the flavor. Then add the sausage to the pot of vegetables. Simmer along, tasting every so often. The important thing is the murky-sharp union of bean-liquor and sausage-juice with tomato-tang and collard-greenery."

SERVINGS *depend on the size of the pot*

Red beans
Tomatoes
Collard greens
Onions
Chorizo, kielbasa, or Italian sausage

Curried Parsnip Soup

GEORGEANNE ROUSSEAU

This is a particularly fresh and deeply flavored starter for a winter meal. It also makes good use of that much underused and underappreciated vegetable, the humble parsnip. The parsnip's sweet, intriguing flavor does well in purées which nicely complement roasts and other hearty beef dishes. A gem among root vegetables, it deserves more of our enthusiasm.

SERVES 8

Curry powder:
1 heaping tablespoon coriander seed
1 level teaspoon cumin seed
1 rounded teaspoon ground turmeric
1 teaspoon ground fenugreek

Soup:
1 medium onion, chopped
1 large clove of garlic, chopped
1 large parsnip, peeled and chopped
2-1/2 tablespoons butter
1 tablespoon flour
4 cups beef stock, heated (homemade preferred)
2 cups heavy cream
Chopped chives and parsley for garnish

To make the curry powder:
Buzz the ingredients together in an electric coffee mill. (If you use the regular coffee mill in which you grind your coffee beans, be sure to clean it out thoroughly after making the curry.) Use 1 tablespoon of the curry powder in the soup and store the remainder in an airtight jar.

To make the soup:
Cook the onion, garlic, and parsnip in the butter in a covered pan for about 10 minutes or until soft but not browned. Stir in the flour and 1 tablespoon of the curry powder. Cook for 2 minutes, stirring occasionally. Gradually add the beef stock, mixing initially with a wire whisk, and cook uncovered until the parsnip is quite soft.

Purée in a food processor or a blender. Reheat the soup, add the cream just before serving, and warm to the proper eating temperature. Sprinkle with chives and parsley and serve.

24

Curried Pumpkin Soup

THE ROSEBOROUGH GRILL

This flavorful soup, featuring fall produce, would be a delicious beginning to a festive Thanksgiving dinner.

Melt the butter in a large saucepan and sauté the onion, celery, and apple over medium heat until tender.

Add the flour and curry powder and blend well; continue to sauté for about 3 minutes, taking care not to let the mixture burn.

Add the chicken broth, cloves, cinnamon, and salt, and stir well. Bring to a simmer and cook uncovered for 30 minutes.

Strain the broth into a clean saucepan and discard the onion, celery, and apple. Return to the heat and whisk in the pumpkin until smooth. Bring to a simmer; add the half-and-half and heat through.

Serve hot with a garnish of chopped parsley.

SERVES 8 to 12

1/2 cup butter
2 onions, chopped
4 stalks of celery, chopped
2 Granny Smith apples, chopped
4 tablespoons flour
6 tablespoons curry powder
8 cups chicken broth
1/8 teaspoon ground cloves
1/8 teaspoon ground cinnamon
2 teaspoons salt, or more to taste
4 cups canned pumpkin
2 cups half-and-half
Chopped parsley for garnish

Butternut Squash & Cider Soup

CANYON RANCH IN THE BERKSHIRES

*Squash and apples are signs that fall has arrived—
and this delicious soup blends them in a delightful combination. It is a full-flavored,
creamy soup but without the usual fat calories.*

SERVES 4

1 shallot, minced
1 clove of garlic,
  minced
1 pound butternut
  squash, peeled and
  cubed
1/2 cup chicken stock
3/4 cup apple cider
1/4 cup lowfat sour
  cream
1/2 red Rome or
  Delicious apple,
  finely diced, for
  garnish
Cracked black pepper

In a medium saucepan, sauté the shallot and garlic, being careful not to burn.

Add the butternut squash and chicken stock and cook until soft enough to blend. Place into a blender container.

Add the remaining ingredients, except the cider, sour cream, and apple, and blend until smooth. Add the cider and sour cream and continue blending until well mixed.

Serve warm in individual soup bowls, garnished with diced apples and a pinch of cracked pepper.

Butternut Spinach Soup

MARTIN'S RESTAURANT

This light, nutritious vegetarian soup lets the flavor of the vegetables shine in their natural glory. For a completely nondairy soup, omit the butter and simply combine and simmer all the vegetables in the water.

Melt the butter in a large pot. Add the onion, celery, and carrots, and cook slowly for about 5 minutes without burning.

Add the squash, potato, bay leaf, salt and white pepper to taste, and water to cover. Simmer until the vegetables are done. Remove the bay leaf.

Purée all the vegetables in a blender, adding water as necessary for proper consistency. Reheat the soup and add the chopped spinach just before serving.

SERVES 6 to 8

2 tablespoons butter
1 Spanish onion, diced
2 stalks celery, diced
2 carrots, diced
1 butternut squash, peeled, seeded, and diced
1 large potato, peeled and diced
1 bay leaf
Salt and white pepper
Water to cover
2 cups fresh spinach, washed and finely chopped

SOUPS

Corn Chowder

TAFT FARMS

Fields where "the corn is high as an elephant's eye" are right here in the Berkshires. Corn from Taft Farms—and from many other local farms—is grown without chemical pesticides. Get your local sweet corn as close to cooking time as possible for maximum flavor.

SERVES 12

1 cup unsalted butter
1/2 cup chopped onion
1 cup chopped celery
1/2 cup chopped green pepper
1/4 cup chopped red pepper
2 cups potatoes, peeled and cut into 1/2-inch cubes
4 cups water
1/2 teaspoon salt (optional)
1/4 teaspoon white pepper
1/4 teaspoon paprika
1/4 teaspoon grated nutmeg
6 tablespoons flour
4 cups whole milk
4 cups cooked corn, cut off the cob
Chopped parsley for garnish
Nutmeg for garnish (optional)

In a large skillet, melt the butter and sauté the onion, celery, green pepper, and red pepper until the onions are golden brown. Transfer to a large, heavy pot.

Add the potatoes, water, salt if desired, pepper, and paprika. Simmer for about 45 minutes or until the potatoes are tender.

Combine the flour with half of the milk in a container with a tight-fitting lid. Cover and shake vigorously until all the flour is blended with the milk. (Or place the milk and flour into a blender container and blend until mixed.)

Immediately but slowly stir the milk mixture into the simmering pot. Continue to stir and bring to almost boiling. Add the remaining milk and the corn. Heat thoroughly but do not boil.

Serve garnished with chopped parsley, and more nutmeg if desired.

Gazpacho

*This is an excellent soup for the summer gardener: it makes use of vegetables
bursting with summer flavor. This soup contains no dairy products
and is perfect to take along for a picnic on a hot day.*

With the chopping blade in the food processor, finely dice all the vegetables. Transfer to a large bowl.

Add the remaining ingredients and mix well.

Refrigerate for 2 to 3 hours before serving. Slice the reserved half cucumber and float the slices in the soup.

SERVES 12

1/2 pound green bell peppers
1 pound carrots
1/2 pound tomatoes
1-1/2 pound cucumbers (reserve one half cucumber for garnish)
3/4 pound celery
1/4 pound red onions
1 cup chopped spinach
1/2 teaspoon celery salt
1 tablespoon salt
1/2 tablespoon pepper
1 teaspoon Tabasco Sauce
1 cup oil
1 cup white vinegar
3 large cans V-8 juice
1 tablespoon Worcestershire sauce
1/4 teaspoon cayenne pepper

SOUPS

29

Strawberry Lemon Soup

THE ELM COURT INN

*A refreshing cold soup to make when the strawberry season is at its peak
in the Berkshires and the local farm markets offer just-picked berries. Many farms,
such as Taft Farms and the Corn Crib, also offer a pick-your-own option: a terrific
outing with the kids, but bring along some sunblock and mosquito repellent!*

SERVES 6

2 large lemons
1 lime
2 pints very ripe
   strawberries
1/4 cup sugar
16 ounces yogurt (plain
   or vanilla)
16 ounces light cream
   or half-and-half
Whipped cream for
   garnish
Mint leaves for garnish
2 lemons, cut into
   wedges, for garnish

Juice the 2 large lemons and the lime. Set aside.

Wash and hull the strawberries. Put them into a blender with the sugar, lemon juice, lime juice, yogurt, and light cream. Blend at high speed. Strain and chill.

Serve in soup bowls, garnished with a dollop of whipped cream, a mint leaf, and the lemon wedges.

Cold Blueberry Soup

THE RED LION INN

*A wonderful soup as an appetizer, or as a light lunch served with fresh fruit,
Brie, warm French bread, and a fruity Beaujolais.*

In a saucepan, combine the 12 ounces of blueberries with the water and Burgundy. Bring to a boil and simmer for 10 minutes. Cool slightly.

Process until smooth in a food processor. Bring the mixture back to a boil.

Dissolve the cornstarch in the water and whisk into the blueberry mixture until thick, approximately 3 minutes. Add the cinnamon, salt, sugar, orange zest, and orange juice.

Chill over an ice bath, or for several hours in the refrigerator, until well chilled. Add the crème de cassis, yogurt, buttermilk, light cream, and the pint of fresh blueberries. Chill well.

Meanwhile, place soup cups into the freezer.

Spoon the soup into the frozen soup cups and garnish with mint leaves.

YIELDS 10 to 12 cups

12 ounces frozen or
  fresh blueberries
1-1/2 cup water
3/4 cup Burgundy
1 tablespoon cornstarch
2 tablespoons water
1/4 teaspoon cinnamon
1/8 teaspoon salt
6 tablespoons sugar
1/2 tablespoon orange
  zest
1/4 cup orange juice
1/2 cup crème de cassis
1-1/2 cup plain yogurt
1/2 cup buttermilk
1/2 cup light cream
1 pint fresh blueberries
Mint leaves for garnish

BRUNCH
& LUNCH

Sweet Potato Pancakes

ENCORE! ENCORE!

This is a variation on the classic potato latke. Latkes are traditionally served during Hanukkah, the Jewish festival that celebrates the miracle of a single small jug of oil keeping a flame burning for eight days. In memory of that jug of oil, it is customary to eat fried foods during Hanukkah. These pancakes are good during the rest of the year as well: try them for brunch, or as a light lunch with some soup.

Grate the potatoes coarsely by hand or in a food processor. Steam over boiling water for 2 minutes; refrigerate immediately.

Sauté the onion and raisins in 1 tablespoon butter till soft. Place into a bowl and refrigerate.

When ready to make the pancakes, mix the potatoes, onion, raisins, eggs, cream, flour, sugar, and cinnamon. If the mixture looks as though it might fall apart, add a little more flour.

Melt the 1/2 cup butter in a very large frying pan. Divide the potato mixture into four pancakes and sauté in the butter over medium heat until golden brown.

These pancakes may be made ahead of time and reheated in the oven at 350°.

SERVES 4

1 pound sweet potatoes, peeled
1/2 cup diced onion
1/2 cup raisins
1 tablespoon butter
2 eggs, lightly whipped
1 cup heavy cream
1 cup flour
1/4 cup sugar
1 tablespoon cinnamon
1/2 cup butter

Apple Pancakes

MARTIN'S RESTAURANT

"One of my customers says that she has eaten pancakes all over the world and considers mine to be world-class pancakes," says Martin Lewis. Martin's Restaurant owes its loyal breakfast and lunch clientele to a first-class chef in the kitchen, Martin himself.

SERVES 6 to 8

6 firm apples
2 tablespoons butter
2 tablespoons brown
    sugar
1 teaspoon vanilla
1 teaspoon cinnamon
1 teaspoon nutmeg
1-1/2 cup flour
1 teaspoon salt
3 tablespoons sugar
1-3/4 teaspoon
    double-acting baking
    powder
2 eggs, beaten
3 tablespoons butter,
    melted
1-1/3 cup milk
Maple syrup on the
    side

Peel, core, and slice the apples. In a frying pan, melt the 2 tablespoons butter and sauté the apples until soft. Add the brown sugar, vanilla, cinnamon, and nutmeg. Let the mixture cool while you prepare the batter.

In a large bowl, mix the flour, salt, sugar, and baking powder. In a separate bowl, whisk together the eggs, melted butter, and milk.

Mix the liquid ingredients into the dry ingredients until just combined (do not overbeat). Add the apple mixture and combine.

Butter and heat a griddle and bake the pancakes until they are brown on both sides.

Serve with maple syrup on the side.

BEST RECIPES OF BERKSHIRE CHEFS

Farmers' Market Apple French Toast

WENDY JENSEN

*This is the dish everybody wanted the recipe for when it was served
at a Great Barrington Farmers' Market meeting. It can also be made with peaches
or blueberries. The apples, peaches, berries, bread, and eggs are all fresh at the Farmers'
Market. Farmer Wendy Jensen can also be found there with her fine fresh produce.*

In a saucepan, heat the brown sugar and butter until they are melted. Add the apples, water, and cinnamon, and cook till the apples are slightly soft. Pour into a 9x13-inch pan. Cover with the bread slices.

In a bowl, mix together the eggs, milk, and vanilla. Pour this mixture over the bread. Cover and refrigerate overnight.

Bake, uncovered, in a preheated oven at 350° for 40 minutes.

SERVES 4 to 6

1/2 cup brown sugar
1/4 cup butter
4 cups sliced apples
2 tablespoons water
1 teaspoon cinnamon
6 to 8 slices Berkshire
   Mountain Bakery
   raisin bread
5 eggs
1-1/2 cup milk
1 tablespoon vanilla

Scrambled Tofu

MARTIN'S RESTAURANT

Tofu is a magical ingredient: it adds protein but very little fat. It has almost no taste of its own but will absorb the flavors of the other ingredients in the dish. This tofu preparation is flavorful and nutritious, and low in calories.

SERVES 4 to 6

Olive oil
1 Spanish onion, sliced
1 green pepper, sliced
8 mushrooms, sliced
1 carrot, julienned
1 zucchini, julienned
1 cup spinach, washed
   and chopped
1 clove garlic, minced
2 blocks of tofu, 1
   pound each, mashed
   or diced
2 tablespoons tamari

Heat some olive oil in a frying pan and sauté the onion and green pepper. When the onion turns transparent, add the mushrooms, carrot, zucchini, spinach, garlic, and tofu. You might also add other colorful vegetables as available— such as tomatoes, broccoli, or string beans.

Cook until heated through. Add the tamari and serve.

BEST RECIPES OF BERKSHIRE CHEFS

Oatmeal Blueberry Soufflé

SEEKONK PINES INN

*According to innkeepers Linda and Chris Best, "This is our favorite recipe
and, judging from our guests' comments, it's theirs too." This unusual dish is often
served as part of the inn's full country breakfast. The inn's building dates from 1832,
and is set in a little valley once known by the local Native Americans as
"the place of the wild goose."*

Soak the oats in the milk overnight.

In the morning, oil a 1-1/2 quart soufflé dish.

Preheat the oven to 325°.

Heat the oatmeal until thick (about 4 minutes in the microwave). Add the cream cheese and stir until melted. Add the sweeteners and spices and stir.

Fold in the stiffly beaten egg whites and the nuts and blueberries.

Pour into the prepared soufflé dish and bake at 325° for 40 minutes.

Serve immediately.

SERVES 4 to 6

3/4 cup quick cooking
   oatmeal
1 cup skim milk
Oil for the soufflé dish
1/3 cup "lite" cream
   cheese
1/4 cup light brown
   sugar or Sucanat
   (available in health
   food stores)
1/4 cup maple syrup
1/4 teaspoon nutmeg
1/2 teaspoon cinnamon
3 egg whites, stiffly
   beaten
1/2 cup chopped
   hazelnuts
1 cup blueberries

Frittata with Pasta, Tomato, Basil & Three Cheeses

THE WRIGHT PASTA COMPANY

Different cheeses and vegetables can be substituted, and plain or flavored pasta can be used in this flexible dish. The Wright Pasta Company currently offers seventeen imaginative pasta flavors, including lemon, sage, tomato basil, and lime cilantro; and more are being added. "The flavors are all natural, and the flour is 100% semolina as behooves a fine quality pasta," explains owner Jeannette Wright.

SERVES 4 to 6

1-1/2 teaspoon olive oil, divided

1/2 medium onion, sliced thin

2 to 3 tomatoes, coarsely chopped

10 fresh basil leaves, julienned

8 eggs

1/4 cup cream or milk

6 ounces fresh pasta

4 ounces mozzarella, coarsely grated

4 ounces cheddar, coarsely grated

2 ounces Parmesan, coarsely grated

Salt and pepper

Preheat the oven to 350°.

Coat a 5x9-inch baking dish with 1/2 teaspoon of the olive oil.

Sauté the onion in the remaining 1 teaspoon olive oil until tender. Add the tomatoes and basil. Toss; remove from the heat and set aside.

In a separate bowl, lightly beat the eggs and the cream. Set aside.

Loosely arrange the fresh pasta in the prepared baking dish.

Spoon the tomato-onion-basil mixture over the pasta. Then layer the cheeses on top. Pour the egg mixture evenly over all.

Bake at 350° for 30 to 35 minutes or until firm in the center.

White Bean Chili with Grilled Chicken

THE ROSEBOROUGH GRILL

Chef Laura Shack says that her goal is to provide diners at the Roseborough Grill with "comfort food—the way you would do it at home if you had the time." The atmosphere is comfortable and charming, too, with roses everywhere. The tables are adorned with dried rose arrangements (made by the chef's mother), painted roses decorate the barstools and wainscoting, and antique rose prints bedeck the forest green and warm pink walls.

Broil the chicken for 10 minutes on each side. Dice or cut into strips. Set aside.

Place the remaining ingredients, except the salt and the garnish, into a large pot, bring to a boil, and simmer for 2 to 3 hours. Add more chicken broth or water if needed.

Add salt to taste.

Add the diced chicken, and garnish with scallions or red onion.

SERVES 8 to 12

4 boneless chicken breasts
6 cups chicken broth
3 cups navy beans
3 teaspoons ground cumin
1 teaspoon oregano
8-ounce can green chilies, diced
2 teaspoons minced garlic
1 cup chopped onions
1 teaspoon white pepper
1/2 teaspoon ground cloves
Salt
Sliced scallions or diced red onion for garnish

Herb Yellowfin Tuna with Warm Pepper Salad

CRANWELL RESORT & HOTEL

This is a very quick dish to make, with a very elegant result. It's ideal for a summer lunch on Cranwell's terrace (or yours), served with a glass of crisp white wine. The tuna steak should be very fresh so that it can be served fairly rare, with the delicate taste of the fresh fish evident.

SERVES 1

Fresh lemon wedge
1/4 pound yellowfin tuna steak
1/2 teaspoon each chopped fresh tarragon and cilantro
1/4 teaspoon cracked black pepper
3 baby heads of mixed organic greens
1 tablespoon olive oil
1/2 tablespoon finely chopped shallots
1/4 cup Chardonnay
1/4 cup balsamic vinegar
6 tablespoons fresh orange juice
1/4 green pepper, sliced
1/4 yellow pepper, sliced
1/4 red pepper, sliced
3 medium shiitake mushrooms
Fresh herbs for garnish

Preheat the oven to 350°.

Drizzle the juice of the lemon wedge over the tuna steak. Rub with the tarragon, cilantro, and pepper. Set aside.

Wash and dry the baby lettuce leaves and arrange them on a serving plate.

In a sauté pan, heat the olive oil. Sauté the tuna for 1 to 2 minutes on each side.

Transfer the tuna to a sizzle pan, pour the Chardonnay over it, and bake at 350° for 3 to 5 minutes (for a rare to medium steak).

Deglaze the sauté pan with the oil remaining in the pan and the wine from the sizzle pan until the liquid is reduced by half. Add the balsamic vinegar and again reduce by half. Add the orange juice and cook for 1 minute.

Add the green, yellow, and red peppers and cook for a little, but do not let the peppers lose their color or firmness.

Arrange the peppers over the greens and pour the sauce over. Place the tuna on top and garnish with fresh herbs.

Elizabeth's South-of-the-Border Polenta

ELIZABETH'S RESTAURANT

*"Polenta breeds fierce loyalties. You love it or you hate it, but you never ignore it,"
says Tom Ellis, the dynamic and personable cook at Elizabeth's.
This Pittsfield eatery is full of surprises and delights, from the neon sign outside
to the menu. Elizabeth's serves delicious Italian food the way it ought to be—
even the simplest of dishes is a delight to the eye and the palate.*

Polenta is made by touch, so these instructions are but a guide.

Bring the water and salt to a boil. Gradually add the cornmeal while stirring continuously with a wooden spoon. "A metal spoon insults the polenta, so be sure you have a sturdy wooden utensil handy," warns cook Tom Ellis. Continue to add cornmeal gradually until the mixture has the consistency of a thick but still moist oatmeal.

Add the remaining ingredients and continue stirring over low heat until the added ingredients are well blended and the polenta is quite thick.

It may now be eaten as is with a touch of sauce, or cooled, sliced, and baked "beneath a conspiracy of cheeses" (as they do at Elizabeth's).

SERVES 15 to 20

2 quarts water
1 tablespoon salt
2 pounds Italian corn meal, ground for polenta
1 cup milk
1 cup grated Parmesan cheese
3 fresh jalepeños, sliced thin

Irish Soda Bread

THE WEATHERVANE INN

*Irish soda bread is an ideal choice for the first-time bread baker: since it contains
no yeast it does not have to rise or be kneaded. It makes good use of buttermilk,
a sometimes underrated ingredient. Despite its name, buttermilk is not high in fat.
Traditionally it was the milk from which the butter was drawn and which was soured
in the churning process. Nowadays it is a cultured skim milk product,
best described as a thin yogurt.*

SERVES 10

4 cups flour
1 teaspoon baking soda
2 teaspoons baking
  powder
1/2 cup butter, softened
1 cup sugar
2 eggs
1-1/4 cup buttermilk
1 tablespoon caraway
  seed
1 cup raisins
2 teaspoons sugar

Preheat the oven to 350°.

Butter and flour a deep round 4-quart cast-iron Dutch oven and set it aside.

Combine all the ingredients, except the last 2 teaspoons sugar, and mix until well blended. The batter will be stiff.

Place the batter into the prepared Dutch oven. With a knife, cut a 1/4-inch-deep cross about 4 inches long on the top of the batter; this will help the bread to cook through. Sprinkle the 2 reserved teaspoons of sugar on the top.

Bake at 350° for 1 hour. Cool for 15 minutes and remove the bread from the pot. Cool completely on a wire rack.

Semolina Bread

CRANWELL RESORT & HOTEL

Built in 1892, the first Berkshire "cottage" designed in the Tudor style, Cranwell has undergone the usual vicissitudes, and was for many years a well-known Jesuit school for boys. It has been restored in recent years to its original splendor, and is notable also for its sweeping views of the South Berkshire hills. The principal dining room, called the Wyndhurst in memory of Cranwell's original name, is open during the summer and fall, and features "fine, not fussy" cuisine prepared under the direction of executive chef Tim Cardillo. Hotel guests in other seasons dine less formally in the Music Room Lounge.

MAKES 10 *loaves*

5 pounds high gluten or all-purpose flour
5 pounds semolina flour
1/2 cup salt
3/4 cup dried rosemary
3/4 cup anise or fennel seed
1 cup pine nuts
3 pints warm water
7 ounces dry yeast
3/4 cup sugar
Oil
Egg wash, made from 1 egg mixed with 1 teaspoon water

In a large bowl, combine the flours, salt, spices, and pine nuts. Mix well.

In a separate bowl, combine the water, sugar, and yeast. Wait until the yeast foams (5 to 10 minutes) and then add it to the flour mixture. Mix well and knead for 5 minutes.

Oil a bowl and place the dough into it. Cover loosely with a piece of plastic wrap and let stand in a warm place, out of a draft, for about 30 minutes or until doubled in size.

Punch down, and form into 10 loaves. Brush the egg wash over the loaves and allow them to rise again for about 30 minutes or until doubled in size.

Preheat the oven to 350°.

Bake the loaves at 350° for 25 to 35 minutes or until they sound hollow when tapped on the bottom.

Morning Glory Muffins

BERKSHIRE COUNTRY DAY SCHOOL SPRING FAIR PANTRY SHELF

*Every May, Berkshire Country Day School hosts a Spring Fair to raise money
for a scholarship program. Preparations for the fair's "Pantry Shelf" involve BCD
parents many days before the event in their famous "bake-ins" at each others' homes.
These muffins are a favorite: foolproof even at high altitudes.*

YIELDS 12 or more muffins

1/2 cup raisins
2 cups flour
1 cup sugar
2 teaspoons baking
   soda
2 teaspoons cinnamon
1/2 teaspoon salt
   (optional)
2 cups grated carrots
1 large, tart apple,
   peeled and grated
1/2 cup sliced almonds
1/2 cup sweetened
   shredded coconut
3 eggs
2/3 cup vegetable oil
2 teaspoons vanilla

Preheat the oven to 350°.

Soak the raisins in hot water for 30 minutes. Drain.

In a large mixing bowl, combine the flour, sugar, baking soda, cinnamon, and salt if desired. Stir in the raisins, carrots, apple, almonds, and coconut.

In a separate bowl, beat the eggs; add the oil and vanilla. Add to the flour mixture and stir until just combined.

Pour the batter into buttered muffin tins. Bake at 350° for 20 to 25 minutes until golden brown.

Apple Juice–Sweetened Muffins

THE BERKSHIRE COFFEE ROASTING COMPANY

*A favorite Great Barrington gathering place, the Berkshire Coffee Roasting Company
is the perfect setting for meeting friends and for people-watching—
especially while enjoying a cup of superb BCRC coffee, and one of these muffins.*

Preheat the oven to 350°.

In a large bowl, sift together the first five ingredients and add the bran.

In a pan, melt the two butters. Add the oil.

In another large bowl, combine the yogurt and the apple juice concentrate and mix with an electric mixer.

In a third bowl, beat the eggs with the electric mixer.

Add the butter and oil mixture to the yogurt mixture and beat with the electric mixer until combined. Add the eggs and mix again. Add the soaked raisins with their water, an additional cup of water, and the apples, and beat with the electric mixer for 30 seconds.

Add the wet mixture to the dry mixture and mix well, but gently, until all the ingredients are just moistened.

Spoon the batter into muffin tins and bake at 350° for 35 minutes.

YIELDS 3 dozen muffins

14 cups organic white flour
3 tablespoons plus 1 teaspoon double-acting baking powder
2 tablespoons cinnamon
2 tablespoons coriander
3 teaspoons sea salt
1/2 cup wheat bran
1/2 cup oat bran
1/2 cup unsalted butter
1/2 cup salted butter
1-2/3 cups canola oil
4 cups (32 ounces) lowfat plain yogurt
2 cans (12 ounces each) frozen apple juice concentrate, thawed
8 eggs
1 cup organic raisins, soaked in 1 cup warm water for 10 minutes
4 cups chopped unsulphured dried apples

Popovers

THE WILLIAMSVILLE INN

Handsomely set in the valley of the Williams River, this excellent New England inn is appreciated for its charm and intimacy, its warmth and comfort, as well as for its cuisine. But there is more—under vivacious owner Gail Ryan, the Williamsville has become a wellspring of Berkshire artistic life. The summer sculpture exhibit, author readings, storyteller presentations, and the occasional "mystery" evening—all featuring Berkshire authors and artists—have endeared the inn to discerning locals and loyal visitors alike.

SERVES 8 to 10

4 extra large eggs
2 cups whole milk
1/8 cup vegetable oil
2 teaspoons vanilla
Pinch of salt
1 cup flour
Butter for the popover
   pans

Preheat the oven to 375°.

Place the unbuttered popover pans into the oven. It is vital to the success of the popovers that the oven and the pans are good and hot before you put in the batter.

Have all the ingredients at room temperature.

Lightly mix together the eggs, milk, oil, vanilla, and salt. Add the flour and blend until just incorporated: do not overmix.

Remove the preheated pans from the oven and, very carefully, butter them well. Fill the cups almost to the top with the batter.

Bake at 375° for 40 to 50 minutes or until the crowns are golden brown, never opening the oven door during the first 30 minutes of baking.

Remove from the pans immediately.

BEST RECIPES OF BERKSHIRE CHEFS

Hot Mulled Cider

BARTLETT'S ORCHARD

On 52 acres in scenic Richmond, Bartlett's Orchard is a Berkshire institution. The orchard's store offers several varieties of apples, Bartlett's own cider and homemade apple treats, and a selection of gourmet food items. The delightful fragrance of apples and cinnamon permeating the store will be recreated in your kitchen in the preparation of this recipe.

Tie up the spices in a small square of cheese cloth, or place them into a tea ball.

Combine the cider, and the brown sugar if desired, in a pot. Add the tied spices. Slowly bring to a boil; cover and simmer for 20 minutes.

Remove the spices, and serve hot.

Variation: Omit the cloves from the spice bag. Instead, stud 2 oranges generously with cloves, then cut the oranges in half. Add the orange halves to the cider at the same time as the spices.

MAKES 10 servings

1 teaspoon allspice
  berries
1 teaspoon whole cloves
3 inches stick cinnamon
Dash nutmeg
2 quarts apple cider
2 tablespoons brown
  sugar (optional)

ENTRÉES

Hachée

FREDI HUNGATE

"This traditional Dutch dish is served with mashed potatoes. I learned how to make it while working in the Netherlands in a small bistro, where I cooked, waited table, and bartended, usually simultaneously and often in five languages! Hachée recipes date from medieval times, and later featured cloves and nutmeg imported from Dutch colonial plantations in Indonesia."

Trim the excess fat off the meat and cut the meat into bitesize pieces.

Divide the margarine between two heavy-bottomed frying pans and fry the meat and the onions separately. The meat should be fried until very well browned on all sides. The onions should become golden brown.

Turn the meat and the onions into a heavy casserole and set onto a low flame. Add just enough water to cover, and add the spices. Simmer, covered, for about 2 hours, or until the onions have just about disintegrated.

If the sauce is too thin at the end of the cooking period, you may thicken it. To do this, combine the cornstarch and water in a cup. Mix well until all the cornstarch is suspended in the water, and add immediately to the broth. Bring to a boil while stirring, and cook for 2 minutes. The sauce should be clear and glossy, not cloudy and white.

SERVES 4 to 6

1 pound stew meat
3 coarsely chopped onions
2 tablespoons margarine
Water
2 bay leaves
2 cloves
1/4 teaspoon nutmeg
Salt and pepper
2 tablespoons cornstarch (if needed)
1/4 cup water (if needed)

Beef & Vegetable Stew

JOE'S DINER

Joe's Diner was immortalized in Norman Rockwell's 1958 Saturday Evening Post cover illustration of a runaway boy and a sympathetic policeman. The diner has been an institution in Lee since Joe Sorrentino took it over in 1955, when he came back from a tour of duty as an Army cook. Joe's friendly atmosphere and down-home cooking attract locals, politicians, and movie stars—and keep them coming back for more. As Berkshire resident Gene Shalit observed, Joe's Diner is a place where "I never saw anyone scowl."

SERVES 8

4 pounds sirloin tips of beef
3 teaspoons oil
1/2 cup flour
12 to 16 cups beef stock
1 clove garlic, minced
Pinch of basil
Pinch of oregano
Salt and pepper
12 potatoes, cut into chunks
4 carrots, sliced thick
2 stalks of celery, sliced
1 large onion, cut into wedges
2 parsnips, sliced
3 tomatoes, cut into wedges

Trim the fat off the beef and cut it into 1-inch cubes.

In a large pot, heat the oil and add the beef, garlic, and seasonings. Sear on all sides over high heat for 4 to 5 minutes. Sprinkle flour over the beef, mix well, and cook over low heat for 5 to 6 minutes.

Pour the beef stock over the meat, stir, and bring to a boil.

Add the vegetables, stir, return to a boil, and lower the heat. Simmer for 2 hours.

Roast Beef with Mushrooms & Feta Cheese

MIRIAM JACOBS

*This is a quick and easy way to get something elegant on the table fast.
If you buy the roast beef and the mushrooms sliced, you can cut the cooking
time for this dish down to about 10 minutes. The feta and lemon juice
give this dish a vaguely Greek flavor. This dish is especially good over rice or with
chunks of bread to sop up the gravy. A simple tomato salad completes the meal.*

In a frying pan, heat the oil. Add the onions and garlic and cook over medium heat until the onions become transparent. Add the mushrooms and cook until they are soft and all their released liquid has cooked down.

Add the lemon juice and feta cheese and stir until the cheese is melted. Add the capers and roast beef. Heat until the beef is warmed through.

Grind fresh pepper over the top. Garnish with the parsley.

SERVES 4

2 tablespoons olive oil
1 onion, chopped
2 cloves of garlic, minced
10 ounces of mushrooms, sliced
Juice of 1/2 lemon
4 ounces feta cheese
1 pound rare roast beef, thickly sliced
2 tablespoons capers
Freshly ground pepper
2 tablespoons minced parsley for garnish

Veal & Shiitake Roulades
with Port Wine Glaze

TRUFFLES & SUCH

*Behind the glass brick façade of Truffles & Such, the clean lines and cool tones
of the Art Deco interior offer the perfect setting for a light lunch, a full dinner,
or an afternoon treat. On the walls are a varied and accomplished collection
of paintings by local artists in the Pittsfield Art League.*

SERVES 6

Duxelles:
6 tablespoons butter
1/4 cup minced
   scallion
1/4 cup minced shallot
1 teaspoon garlic
4 ounces shiitake
   mushrooms, minced
4 mushrooms, minced
1 teaspoon A-1 Sauce

Tomato coulis:
2 tablespoons butter
1 teaspoon minced
   garlic
1 cup tomatoes
1/4 teaspoon thyme

To make the duxelles:
In a frying pan over low heat, melt the butter and add the scallion, shallot, garlic, shiitakes, and mushrooms. Keep the heat low, and "sweat" the ingredients until the shallot is transparent and the ingredients have softened. Add the A-1 Sauce, stir, and continue to cook until all the liquid has evaporated. Cool completely before using. Duxelles may be made ahead of time.

To make the tomato coulis:
Plunge the tomatoes for a minute or two into a big pot of boiling water, remove from the water, and peel, seed, and dice. In a saucepan over low heat, melt the butter and cook the garlic until golden and fragrant. Add the tomatoes and thyme. Simmer until about half the liquid has evaporated. This coulis may be made ahead of time and reheated.

To prepare the veal:
Preheat the oven to 350°.

Cut the veal into three pieces for each serving. Place the pieces of veal between two pieces of wax paper and pound with a flat mallet until very thin.

Distribute the duxelles among the veal pieces. Roll up and place into an oiled baking pan, seam side down. Sprinkle with the julienned leeks. Add a small amount of stock to the pan. Bake at 350° for approximately 20 to 25 minutes.

To make the port wine glaze:
While the veal is baking, combine the port wine and chicken stock in a saucepan and reduce until syrupy.

To serve, reheat the coulis and divide it among 6 plates. Place a portion of veal on each plate, and pour the glaze over.

Veal:
6 portions veal, 4 to 5
    ounces each
1 leek, julienned
Oil for the pan

Port wine glaze:
1-1/2 cup port wine
1-1/2 cup chicken stock

Osso Buco à la Springs

The Italian country folk who couldn't afford "good" cuts of meat got their revenge on this one. The shank of veal, unresponsive to conventional treatment and disdained by the cooks of the gentry, proved marvelously flavorful when patiently browned and braised. Indeed, it is so savory that it enriches and blends beautifully with any number of companions. Today, osso buco is one of the universal favorites of Italian cuisine, whether aristocratic or country style. The Springs version, redolent of wine and enriched with diced ham and many flavorings, is both hearty and refined, an excellent and well-loved example of the many treatments of this classic dish.

SERVES 6

2 veal shinbones, cut
   crosswise into six
   portions
Flour
3 tablespoons oil
3 tablespoons butter
Salt and pepper
1 cup sherry
1 cup Burgundy
8-ounce can tomatoes
3 cups beef stock
1/3 cup ham, chopped
1 onion, chopped
2 cloves garlic, minced
1/2 cup chopped
   carrot
1/2 cup chopped celery
1 teaspoon basil
1/2 teaspoon sage
1 bay leaf
3 sprigs of parsley,
   chopped
12 mushrooms, sliced

Tie the veal portions with string and dredge in flour. In a heavy metal pan, heat the oil and butter and cook the veal until golden brown, adding salt and pepper as desired.

Add the sherry and Burgundy and cook until the liquid is reduced by half. Add the rest of the ingredients except the parsley and the mushrooms. Cover and continue cooking for 3 to 3-1/2 hours.

During the last 5 minutes of cooking, add the parsley and mushrooms to the osso buco. Serve hot, with boiled rice or risotto on the side, and each veal bone topped with a spoonful of gremolata.

To make the gremolata:

While the osso buco is cooking, heat the oil and butter in a small skillet. Add the rest of the ingredients and sauté until the garlic is tender.

Gremolata:

4 tablespoons oil
4 tablespoons butter
4 cloves of garlic, minced
3 tablespoons parsley, chopped
Grated rind of 1 lemon
3 anchovies

Babotie

EMBREE'S RESTAURANT

In the heart of Housatonic, Embree's is inventive, sophisticated, and upbeat. Embree's Babotie is of African parentage, and as upscale as a meatloaf would ever want to get.

SERVES 8

6 slices of stale bread
1/2 cup milk (or slightly more)
3 pounds ground lamb
4 tablespoons curry powder
Pinch of cayenne
Pinch of ground coriander
Freshly ground pepper
6 eggs
1/4 cup chopped parsley
1 cup raisins
4 cloves of garlic, puréed (in a food processor)
1/2 cup dry bread crumbs
8 eggs
1 tablespoon honey
Chutney on the side

Preheat the oven to 350°.

Tear the bread into small pieces, place into a large bowl, and soak in the milk. (Use a bit more milk if the bread is very dry.)

Add the ground lamb, curry powder, cayenne, coriander, three turns of the pepper mill, the 6 eggs, chopped parsley, raisins, garlic, and breadcrumbs. Mix well. Set aside 4 cups of the mix and place the rest into a large meatloaf pan.

In a separate bowl, mix together the 4 cups of reserved mix, the 8 eggs, and the honey. Pour over the top of the meatloaf. Bake at 350° for 15 minutes or until the custard is set. Slice as you would a meatloaf, and serve with chutney on the side.

Pork Medallions with Ginger Pear Coulis

THE EGREMONT INN

Established in 1780 as a stagecoach stop, the Egremont Inn is still offering hospitality in the friendly tavern room, on the wraparound porch for Sunday brunch, or by a warm fire on a cool evening. Many of the inn's delicious dishes are seasoned with herbs right from their own garden.

To make the ginger pear coulis:
Core, peel, and thinly slice the pear. In a small saucepan, melt the butter over moderate heat. Add the pear, ginger root, and cinnamon, and sauté briefly.

Pour the pear brandy over and ignite. Cover tightly and cook over low heat until the pear is tender.

Remove from the heat, purée the mixture, and return it to the pan. Keep heated until ready to use.

To prepare the pork medallions:
Trim any excess fat from the pork cutlets. Season with the salt and pepper and dredge with the flour.

Heat the clarified butter in a sauté pan. Add the pork and sauté on both sides until the meat is well browned and cooked through.

To serve, place a small pool of ginger pear coulis on each plate and center the cutlets on top of the coulis.

SERVES 2

Ginger pear coulis:
1 large Bartlett pear
1 tablespoon butter
1 teaspoon grated
   ginger root
1/4 teaspoon cinnamon
2 tablespoons pear
   brandy

Pork medallions:
4 boneless pork loin
   cutlets, 4 ounces each
Salt and pepper
Flour
2 tablespoons clarified
   butter

Sautéed Loin of Venison
with Papaya Sauce & Potato Rose

CRANWELL RESORT & HOTEL

*This distinctive version of a standard classic was chef Tim Cardillo's entry
in the "Great Chefs of New England" series. It features a rich fruit-flavored marinade
which is then used in the reduction, ensuring a delicious complementarity
between meat and sauce. Hunters and their friends take note:
this dish is reputedly even tastier when prepared with wild local game.*

SERVES 1

Venison:

1/2 cup brandy

2 tablespoons golden raisins

2 tablespoons dark raisins

1/2 tablespoon fresh rosemary

1/4 teaspoon cracked black pepper

1/2 tablespoon minced shallot

5-ounce fresh loin of venison

2 tablespoons olive oil

1/2 cup venison, beef, or veal stock

1/4 dark plum, sliced

Seeds of 1/4 pomegranate

To prepare the venison:

In a large bowl, mix the brandy, the two kinds of raisins, rosemary, pepper, and shallot. Add the venison, turn to cover with the marinade, and let stand for 4 to 6 hours.

Preheat the oven to 350°.

Remove the venison from the marinade and pat dry; reserve the marinade.

In a frying pan, heat the olive oil. Cook the venison on all sides until seared. Remove from the pan and roast at 350° for 10 minutes for rare to medium rare.

Deglaze the pan with the marinade until the liquid is reduced by half. Add the venison stock, dark plum, and pomegranate seeds.

To make the potato rose:

Preheat the oven to 350°.

Lay out the potato slices in a straight line, each slice overlapping the other about half way. Season with the salt, pepper, and chopped parsley.

Roll the potato from the top, starting off tightly and relaxing the roll as you come to the end. Set the potato on end in a small (4-ounce) ramekin. Drizzle with a small amount of oil or clarified butter.

Bake the potato at 350° for 8 to 10 minutes.

To make the papaya sauce:

Combine the papaya and the orange juice and purée them in a blender. Add the chili oil, rosemary, and pepper.

When ready to serve, place into a small saucepan and gently heat until warm.

To prepare the asparagus:

In a skillet, sauté the asparagus in a bit of oil just until bright green and still crisp.

To serve:

Arrange the asparagus spears on a plate in a star pattern, with the potato rose at the center. Cut the venison into 5 slices. Place a spoonful of marinade between each asparagus, and a slice of venison to one side of the sauce. Place a spoonful of the heated papaya sauce on the bottom of each venison slice.

Potato rose:
1 thin, long russet potato, very thinly sliced on a mandoline
Salt
Freshly cracked black pepper
Chopped parsley
Olive oil or clarified butter

Papaya sauce:
1/2 papaya, peeled and diced
1/2 cup fresh orange juice
1/4 teaspoon chili oil
1/4 teaspoon fresh rosemary
1/4 teaspoon cracked black pepper

Asparagus:
5 asparagus spears
Oil

Rabbit Terrine

THE OLD INN ON THE GREEN

*This terrine combines country-style ingredients with a gourmet sensibility.
Admittedly a labor-intensive dish, it results in a spectacular presentation—
and most of the work can be finished ahead of time.*

SERVES 4

Terrine:
1 bottle of white wine
Salt and pepper
1/2 head of red
  cabbage, julienned
8 red peppers
20 shiitake mushrooms
Olive oil
Salt and white pepper
Fresh thyme
4 rabbit legs, bones and
  tendons removed
Olive oil for the terrine
1/2 head of red kale,
  washed and stemmed

Custard:
4 eggs
2-1/2 cups cream
Salt and pepper
2 tablespoons salsify
  purée
2 tablespoons roasted
  garlic purée
Bunch of fresh thyme,
  minced

To prepare the terrine ingredients:
Pour the wine into a large pot, season with salt and pepper, and bring to a boil. Add the cabbage and blanch until almost translucent. Remove the cabbage, drain, and set aside.

One at a time, roast the red peppers on a large skewer over an open flame until the skin is charred. Immediately plunge into cold water. Peel, and wash away any black flakes. Dice the roasted peppers and place into a strainer to drain.

Stem the shiitakes. Sauté the caps in olive oil and season with salt, white pepper, and fresh thyme. When softened, set the mushrooms aside to cool.

In a sauté pan, sauté the rabbit legs in olive oil until they are slightly browned on the outside but still rare on the inside. Set aside. When cool, dice the meat into 1/2-inch pieces.

To make the custard:
Combine the eggs, cream, salt and pepper, salsify purée, roast garlic purée, and thyme, and whisk until well blended.

To assemble the terrine:
Preheat the oven to 375°.

Line a well-oiled terrine with the largest leaves of the red kale, overlapping the leaves and letting some excess hang over the top edge.

Layer the red cabbage evenly over the bottom of the terrine, about 1 inch high. Pour one fifth of the custard over to cover. Pat the custard down evenly.

Layer half the diced rabbit. Pour one fifth of the custard over and pat down.

Layer the diced red peppers. Pour one fifth of the custard over and pat down.

Layer the other half of the diced rabbit. Pour one fifth of the custard over and pat down.

Layer the shiitake caps, alternating them face up and face down. Cover with the remaining one fifth of the custard.

Fold the kale leaves over the top layer. Place the lid on the terrine and cover with aluminum foil. Place in a bain-marie and bake for 1-1/2 to 2 hours at 375°, removing the lid after 30 minutes.

The terrine is finished when the custard is set. Chill the terrine overnight.

To make the sauce:
Reduce the rabbit stock and whip in the butter.

To serve, slice the terrine, pour the sauce over, and garnish with pearl onions.

Sauce:
Rabbit stock
2 tablespoons butter

Pearl onions for garnish

Herb-Infused Baby Pheasant au Jus

THE OLD INN ON THE GREEN

*The same words can be used to describe this dish, the entire menu, and the inn itself—
simple elegance and sophistication. The inn was built as a stagecoach stop
on the colonial road from Hartford to Albany. Then the railroad went elsewhere,
and the New Marlboro Green was left beautifully preserved. The inn's colonial interior
has been reinterpreted with candlelit chandeliers, spare and elegant furnishings,
and whimsical floral arrangements. Accommodations are also available
at Gedney Farm, just down the road: a nineteenth-century gentleman's horse barn
has been converted to original, interesting, and comfortable lodgings.*

SERVES 6

3 young pheasants,
    2-1/2 to 3 pounds
    (reserve carcasses
    and tenderloins)
Salt and pepper
Clarified butter or olive
    oil

Herb stuffing:
6 medium cloves of
    garlic
6 sprigs of fresh thyme
3 sprigs of fresh
    rosemary

Farce:
6 pheasant tenderloins
    (reserved)
1/2 cup cream
2 egg whites
Salt and pepper
Fresh thyme, chopped
1 egg yolk, if needed

To prepare the pheasant:
Debone the pheasants, keeping the breast, thigh, and leg intact. Debone the thigh. French trim the leg and the wing of the breast.

Roast the carcasses at 350° till brown.

To make the herb stuffing:
Chop the ingredients together; reserve.

To make the farce:
In a food processor, purée the reserved tenderloins. Stop the blade and drizzle the cream over the tenderloins. Briefly pulse to mix; do not overpulse or the cream will separate.

In a separate bowl, whip the egg whites until stiff. Fold the pheasant tenderloin mixture into the egg whites. Season with salt and pepper and thyme.

Drop a teaspoon of farce into a small saucepan of simmering water to see if it binds. If not, fold in one egg yolk.

To make the jus:
In a sauté pan, melt the butter and sauté the vegetables with the thyme until tender. Remove the thyme sprig. Place into a large stock pot and add the roasted pheasant carcasses, bay leaves, peppercorns, and bouquet garni. Simmer slowly for 2 hours, skimming frequently.

Strain. In a clean pot, reduce the stock by simmering it down until dark. Season with salt and pepper.

To stuff the pheasants:
Insert your fingers underneath the skin from the back side of the pheasants' breast. Stuff about 1 tablespoon of the herb stuffing between the skin and the breast. Pat the skin down. Spoon the farce into the deboned thigh and close it up with toothpicks.

Season the pheasants with salt and pepper on both sides.

To assemble the dish:
Preheat the oven to 400°.

In a large pan, sauté the pheasants in clarified butter or olive oil until the skin is crisp and brown.

Roast the pheasants at 400° for 10 to 15 minutes or until done.

Slice the breast and thigh and arrange on warmed plates. Garnish each plate with rosemary new potatoes and asparagus and carrot bundles. Pour jus over and serve.

Jus:
3 tablespoons butter
1 cup diced carrot
1 cup diced onion
1 cup diced celery
1 bay leaf, crushed
Sprig of thyme
3 pheasant carcasses (reserved)
2 whole bay leaves
4 peppercorns
Bouquet garni (3 sprigs of parsley, 1/2 bay leaf, 2 sprigs of fresh thyme, and 1 whole clove, tied up together in a square of cheese cloth)
Salt and pepper

ENTRÉES

Chicken Egremont

THE WEATHERVANE INN

A renovated and enlarged eighteenth-century farmhouse, the Weathervane Inn offers relaxed dining by candlelight, with homemade breads and desserts. High ceilings, wide floorboards, and fine craftsmanship throughout the inn create a memorable setting. Chicken Egremont is one of the inn's most popular entrées.

SERVES 4

4 small chicken breasts, boneless
1 box frozen spinach, thawed, or 1 bag fresh spinach, cooked and drained
4 ounces Alouette, Boursin, Rondelé, or any other herbed cream cheese, divided into 8 portions
1/2 cup flour
1/2 teaspoon salt
1/8 teaspoon nutmeg
2 eggs, beaten
1 stack Ritz crackers, crushed
1/4 cup butter

Preheat the oven to 500°.

Split each of the chicken breasts in half. Place the pieces between two layers of plastic wrap or wax paper and pound lightly with a mallet until they are 1/4 inch thick.

Divide the spinach evenly over four of the chicken pieces. Top each with one of the portions of cheese. Place the remaining chicken pieces on top, sandwich fashion, and press down.

Dip each sandwich into the flour combined with the salt and nutmeg, then into the beaten egg, and lastly into the crushed cracker crumbs.

Melt the butter in an ovenproof baking dish large enough to hold the chicken without touching. Place the chicken into the baking dish and bake at 500° for 12 to 15 minutes until the chicken looks lightly browned and is cooked through.

Remove from the oven, place on a serving plate, and top each portion with one of the remaining pieces of cheese.

BEST RECIPES OF BERKSHIRE CHEFS

Chicken & Artichokes

COBBLE CAFÉ

*Owned jointly by the unrelated Smiths, Edward "Ned" and Gerald "Gerry,"
the Cobble Café is comfortable and casual. Serving breakfast, lunch, and dinner
(and, in the summer, lighter fare), enhanced by choice beer and wine, the café features
"a new style, varied American menu. We're moving to lighter food," according to Ned.*

Cut the chicken into serving pieces and dredge with flour. Heat the olive oil in a skillet and sauté the chicken over medium high heat till well browned. Place the chicken into a Dutch oven or a casserole.

In the same skillet, sauté the shallots. Pour the Chablis over the shallots and cook over high heat, scraping the bottom of the skillet, until the liquid is reduced by half.

Pour the can of artichokes and their liquid over the chicken. Pour the wine mixture over the artichokes. Cover and simmer for 2 hours over low heat. Salt and pepper to taste.

Serve the chicken with a sprinkling of lemon juice and spoon some of the sauce over all. Serve at once.

SERVES 4 to 6

Whole frying chicken
  (about 3 pounds)
Flour for dredging
1/2 cup olive oil
1 to 2 shallots, chopped
1-1/4 cup Chablis or
  other dry white wine
1 can artichokes (8 to 10
  count)
Salt and pepper
Juice of 1 lemon

Maple Dijon–Glazed Chicken

CANYON RANCH IN THE BERKSHIRES

*Canyon Ranch, a Tucson, Arizona, luxury spa, has a second home in the Berkshires.
The spa's nineteenth-century mansion, "Bellefontaine," a replica of Le Petit Trianon,
has been restored to glory and then some, with a spectacular resort facility
and guest rooms. This recipe is typical of the haute cuisine, low-cholesterol dining
at Canyon Ranch: it aims to make guests feel pampered, to please the tastebuds,
and to skimp on the calories. Each serving contains approximately 180 calories
and only 5 grams of fat.*

SERVES 4

Maple Dijon glaze:

1/2 cup Dijon mustard

2-1/2 teaspoons white
   wine

1/4 teaspoon
   Worcestershire sauce

Pinch of black pepper

1 teaspoon finely diced
   shallot

2-1/2 teaspoons pure
   maple syrup

4 chicken breast halves,
   boned, skinned, and
   defatted

Prepare coals for grilling, or preheat
the broiler.

To make the maple Dijon glaze:
Combine the ingredients in a small bowl
and blend well.

To grill the chicken:
Grill the chicken until done, brushing
from time to time with the glaze.

BEST RECIPES OF BERKSHIRE CHEFS

Roast Cornish Game Hens
with Spinach Feta Stuffing

WINDFLOWER INN

*Across the street from the golf course of the Egremont Country Club is the Federal-style
mansion of Windflower Inn. Vegetables, herbs, and berries grown in the inn's
organic garden find their way to the table in the growing season.
The inn's cuisine is eclectic, with a country-casual atmosphere.*

Preheat the oven to 350°.

Set the game hens aside.

To make the spinach feta stuffing:
In a frying pan, heat the oil and sauté
the shallot and onion but be sure not to
brown them. Add the diced giblets and
sauté for a few more minutes. Add the
spinach, Marsala, and salt, pepper, and
thyme to taste, and sauté until most of
the liquid is cooked away. Transfer the
spinach mixture to a bowl. Add the rice
and feta cheese and mix well.

To make the basting mixture:
Whisk the ingredients together.

To prepare the game hens:
Stuff the game hens with the spinach
feta stuffing, place them on a rack in a
roasting pan, and salt and pepper them
to taste. Cover with aluminum foil. Roast
at 350° for 30 minutes. Then remove the
foil and roast for 30 minutes more. Baste
every 20 minutes or so with the basting
mixture. Before serving, pour the remaining basting mixture over the game
hens.

SERVES 6

6 Cornish game hens
   (reserve giblets)

Spinach feta stuffing:
2 to 3 tablespoons oil
1 large shallot, minced
1 small onion, minced
Giblets from the game
   hens, diced
2 packages (10-ounce)
   frozen spinach,
   thawed, drained, and
   chopped
Salt and pepper
Thyme
1/4 cup Marsala
1 cup cooked rice
1/2 cup feta cheese,
   crumbled

Basting mixture:
1 cup white wine
Juice of 1 lemon
1 tablespoon melted
   butter
1 teaspoon tarragon

Homard Bouillabaisse
with Aïoli & Garlic Croutons

LA TOMATE BISTRO

It's no surprise that La Tomate, which describes itself as a "Bistro Provençal,"
would offer bouillabaisse, the famous seafood stew from Provence.
La Tomate's version reveals a few surprises: while it contains the traditional saffron,
the fennel flavor comes from the Ricard, and the broth is clear.
The aïoli is also delicious as a dip for vegetables or as a sauce for any cold leftover fish.

SERVES 1

Fish fumet:
Snapper head
Olive oil
1/2 cup onions
1/2 cup tomatoes
1/4 cup celery
1/4 cup carrots
1/4 cup leeks
1/4 cup garlic
Bay leaf
Fresh thyme
1/4 cup Ricard
2 quarts water
2 pinches saffron

Bouillabaisse:
1 lobster, 1 to 1-1/4
    pounds
2 ounces sole
2 ounces monkfish
2 ounces snapper
3 large mussels
2 medium clams
2 cups fish fumet
1 cup white wine

To make the fish fumet:
Crush the snapper head, rinse off the blood, and discard the gills. Sauté in hot olive oil. Add all the vegetables and herbs and the Ricard.

In a stock pot, combine the vegetable mixture, water, and saffron. Cook for 2 hours. Strain the broth and reserve.

To make the bouillabaisse:
Cut the lobster in half and crack the claws. In a skillet, sauté the lobster in hot olive oil. Add two cups of the fish fumet, and the white wine. Add all the fish, clams, and mussels. When the clams open up, the dish is cooked.

To make the aïoli:
Place the egg yolks and mustard into a large bowl. Add the lemon juice, salt and pepper, and Ricard. Add the oil gradually in a small, even stream. Add the saffron. Let the saffron "bleed" for 30 minutes, then stir. Add the chopped garlic.

To make the garlic croutons:
Preheat the oven to 400°.

Brush the bread slices with the garlic oil. Toast at 400° until golden and crisp.

To serve, ladle the bouillabaisse into bowls. Top with the garlic croutons spread with the aïoli.

Aïoli:
2 egg yolks
1/2 cup strong Dijon
   mustard
1/4 cup lemon juice
Salt and pepper
2 tablespoons Ricard
2 cups oil
2 pinches saffron
1/4 cup garlic, chopped

Garlic croutons:
French bread, sliced on
   the diagonal
Garlic oil

Shrimp Wrapped in Prosciutto with Smoked Tomato Sauce

ENCORE! ENCORE!

The Berkshire Hilton Inn's own dining room offers an elegant ambience and sophisticated fare. The smoky flavor of this dish is an unexpected treat.

SERVES 4

20 very thin slices of prosciutto, folded in half lengthwise
20 very large shrimp, peeled and deveined
1/4 cup olive oil

Smoked tomato sauce:
2 cups hickory chips, soaked in water for 1 to 2 hours
5 large tomatoes, cored
1 teaspoon oregano
1 teaspoon chopped garlic
Salt and pepper
1/2 cup cold butter

Preheat the oven to 400°.

Wrap one slice of prosciutto tightly around the very top of each shrimp, as close to the head as possible. Squeeze gently in the palm of your hand to seal.

Dab the prosciutto-wrapped shrimp with the olive oil and place them into a heavy baking pan. Bake at 400° for 5 to 8 minutes until done.

To make the smoked tomato sauce:
Drain the hickory chips and spread them over the bottom of a heavy roasting pan. Cover with a roasting rack.

Core the tomatoes and place them on the rack. Cover tightly. Place the pan onto a stove burner under a hood with the exhaust fan running. Cook over medium high heat for 45 minutes. Remove the tomatoes to a saucepan and add the oregano and garlic. Simmer over low heat for 30 minutes or until nearly dry. Place the tomatoes into a blender or food processor and add the butter, a tablespoon at a time. Serve within one hour.

BEST RECIPES OF BERKSHIRE CHEFS

Alice's Special Shrimp

ALICE BROCK

This dish was created for visual as well as culinary effect, with different shapes and colors, all retaining their own individuality. It turned out to be an all-time favorite at Alice's Restaurant, the famous Berkshire eatery immortalized by the '60s movie of that name, starring Arlo Guthrie and a contingent of Berkshire locals.

Melt the butter in a sauté pan over fairly high heat. Toss in the remaining ingredients, except the orzo, all at once.

Let it all sizzle up, turning the shrimp once, and immediately serve over the orzo the moment the shrimp are cooked. It takes just minutes.

In the restaurant, each portion was cooked to order in its own little pan. Four or so portions can be prepared at a time in a 12-inch or larger pan. The ingredients should not be crowded.

SERVES 1

1 or more tablespoons butter
5 raw jumbo shrimp, shelled and deveined
4 black olives, pitted
4 green olives, pitted
4 ripe cherry tomatoes
3 to 4 artichoke hearts (packed in oil, lightly drained)
1 handful freshly chopped scallions and parsley
1 tablespoon sherry
Generous pinch of crumbled dried tarragon
One portion of cooked orzo

Special Seafood

DOS AMIGOS MEXICAN RESTAURANT

Dos Amigos serves a taste of Mexico in New England. The cheerful interior and child-friendly atmosphere have made it a family favorite for many years. Special Seafood is one of their most popular dishes.

SERVES 18

1 tablespoon oil
1 small onion, chopped
1/2 red bell pepper, chopped
3 pounds shrimp
4 pounds scallops
1/2 pound snow crab legs
1 chicken bouillon cube
1/2 cup butter
1/2 cup flour
1/4 bunch fresh cilantro, chopped
1/2 teaspoon ground cumin
1/2 teaspoon ground coriander

Place the oil in a pan, and sauté the onion and red pepper until soft. Add the shrimp and cook half through. Add the scallops and snow crab legs and cook through.

Take some broth from the seafood and dissolve the chicken bouillon cube.

In a separate pan, melt the butter. Add the flour and stir to make a roux. Stir the broth with the dissolved bouillon cube into the roux. Add the cilantro, cumin, and coriander and stir until creamy.

Add this mixture to the seafood and stir well.

Mahi Mahi with Chanterelle Mushrooms

CANYON RANCH IN THE BERKSHIRES

One of chef Correia's most exciting seafood recipes, this dish is a favorite with the guests at Canyon Ranch. Accompanied by steamed red bliss potatoes, it's easy to prepare.

In a sauté pan, heat the 1 tablespoon oil and sauté the carrot, celery, leek, and shallot until tender. Set aside.

Place a collapsible steamer basket into a medium-size pot and add the water. Place the spinach and chanterelles into the steamer basket, cover the pot, and steam for 2 to 4 minutes.

Combine the vegetable stock, wine, and 1/4 teaspoon olive oil, and heat.

Prepare coals for grilling, or preheat the broiler. Grill or broil the mahi mahi.

Place one fillet over each portion of steamed spinach and chanterelles, and top with the sautéed vegetables.

Ladle 2 tablespoons of the stock mixture over each serving.

SERVES 4

1 tablespoon olive oil
1 medium carrot, finely diced
1 tablespoon finely diced celery
1 tablespoon finely diced leek
1 tablespoon finely diced shallot
2 cups water
1/4 pound fresh spinach
3/4 pound chanterelles
1/2 cup vegetable stock
1/2 teaspoon white wine
1/4 teaspoon olive oil
2 tablespoons chopped chives
4 mahi mahi fillets, 4 ounces each

Spaghetti alla Carbonara

AIDA BARG

*"The day when David, my future husband, asked me to prepare spaghetti for him,
I was as nervous as could be: that was the final test!
I prepared Spaghetti alla Carbonara and Spaghetti alle Zucchine.
The result was that, very soon after, we were married!"
Aida and David founded and directed L'Orchestra in the Berkshires.*

SERVES 4

1/4 pound slab bacon
2 tablespoons olive oil
1 clove of garlic,
   crushed
1 pound spaghetti
3 eggs
Salt and pepper
2 ounces Parmesan
   cheese, freshly grated
2 ounces Romano
   cheese, freshly grated

Cut the bacon into small cubes. In a frying pan, heat the olive oil and add the bacon and crushed garlic. When the bacon is golden brown, remove and discard the garlic.

Cook the spaghetti in lots of boiling salted water, and drain them when they are al dente (about half the time indicated on the package). Add the spaghetti to the bacon, mixing continuously on low heat for a couple of minutes.

Beat the eggs with the salt and pepper and add to the spaghetti with half of the cheese. Mix well.

Serve immediately with the rest of the cheese.

BEST RECIPES OF BERKSHIRE CHEFS

Spaghetti alle Zucchine

AIDA BARG

*Aida's hints for "good pasta, Italian style": Cook pasta in a lot of salty boiling water.
De Cecco is the recommended brand, but if you don't find it, cook pasta for only half
of the time suggested on the box. Do not put oil into the water. Just stir often and don't
overcook, and the pasta will not stick together. If it does, change brands!
Drain the pasta thoroughly and fast, and always keep some of the water to add later
if the pasta becomes dry. This is especially handy if you are not using a tomato sauce.
Don't drain the pasta too long: it will continue to cook and will stick.
Always serve pasta immediately after cooking.*

In a large frying pan, heat the olive oil and add the onion and garlic. Fry until golden brown. Add the zucchini, stir, cover, and cook on a low flame for about 35 minutes. Then add the parsley, and salt and pepper to taste, and cook for 5 minutes longer.

In a lot of salted water, cook the spaghetti al dente. Drain thoroughly and transfer to a bowl. Add the egg yolk and melted butter and mix rapidly.

Add the zucchini and mix again.

Cover the pasta with the Parmesan cheese.

SERVES 4

1/4 cup olive oil
1 onion, minced
1 clove of garlic, minced
6 zucchini, sliced
One bunch of parsley, minced
Salt and pepper
1 pound spaghetti
1 egg yolk
2 tablespoons melted butter
2 ounces Parmesan cheese, freshly grated or sliced

Foil-Wrapped Spaghetti in White Clam Sauce

GEORGEANNE ROUSSEAU

"This method of preparation infuses the pasta with the flavor of the clams in a magical way. Try it with other pastas and sauces!"

SERVES 2

24 to 30 littleneck clams
2 tablespoons olive oil
1 medium clove garlic,
    finely chopped
1/2 teaspoon dried
    thyme or oregano
1 tablespoon cognac
Freshly ground black
    pepper
2 tablespoons finely
    chopped parsley
1/4 teaspoon hot
    pepper flakes
8 ounces spaghetti
Salted water for boiling
    the pasta

Preheat the oven to 500°.

Line a baking dish with a double layer of heavy duty aluminum foil. Form into a well to receive the spaghetti, leaving extra foil to fold into a tight seal.

Open the clams. Drain and strain, reserving 3/4 cup of the clam liquor. Chop the clams and set aside.

In a small pan, heat the oil and add the garlic. Cook briefly without browning; add the reserved clam liquor and the thyme. Bring just to a boil.

Drop the spaghetti into boiling salted water and stir until it becomes limp. Drain quickly and place into the center of the foil-lined baking dish. Add the cognac and freshly ground pepper. Sprinkle with the parsley and hot pepper flakes and add the nearly boiling clam broth and the chopped clams.

Quickly seal the ends of the foil securely, so that the sauce cannot leak and the steam cannot escape. Bake for exactly 10 minutes at 500°. Remove the dish from the oven and cut open the top of the foil. Transfer the pasta to a bowl and serve immediately.

BEST RECIPES OF BERKSHIRE CHEFS

Five-Bean Chili

CHURCH STREET CAFÉ

Church Street Café, in the heart of Lenox, is the ideal spot for rest and refreshment after walking and shopping in downtown Lenox. Airy and light by day, it glows with candlelight in the evening. Eyecatching artwork is displayed on the walls. Clayton Hambrick's excellent cooking is inventive and popular.

Sauté the garlic and onion in the oil until soft. Add the tomatoes and spices. Simmer for 30 minutes.

Add the beans, jalapeño peppers, and cilantro, and simmer for 20 minutes more.

SERVES 8

2 tablespoons minced garlic
2 cups chopped onions
2 tablespoons vegetable oil
4 cups plum tomatoes, crushed
1 tablespoon ground cumin
2 teaspoons salt, adjusted to taste
2 tablespoons good hot chili powder
2 cups each cooked black beans, great Northern beans, black-eyed peas, kidney beans, and pinto beans
1 jalepeño pepper, minced
1/2 cup chopped cilantro

My Brother's Vegetable Curry with Egg

RODELINDE ALBRECHT HANDLER

"When I made this vegetable curry for a recent dinner party, my husband, Jack, (who really knows about food) recommended that I include the recipe here. My brother Christian had taught me how to make it years ago. In spite of the eggs, it is an Indian, not an African, curry; the egg is an Anglo-Indian conceit." Rodelinde is a freelance editor and designer for a variety of publishing projects, including this book.

SERVES 6 or more

2 cans garbanzos (about 15 oueces each), or 4 cups home-cooked plus 1-1/2 cups of their cooking liquid
1/4 cup olive oil
4 cloves of garlic, julienned
3 medium onions, coarsely chopped
1 teaspoon cumin seed (optional)
1 teaspoon brown mustard seed (optional)
3 to 4 tablespoons good quality curry powder
6-ounce can tomato paste
3 cups water
1 head of cauliflower, about 1-1/2 pound, broken into florets
6 medium potatoes, cut into large chunks

Drain the garbanzos and reserve the liquid.

In a large, heavy pot (such as a Dutch oven), heat the olive oil over medium high heat. Add the garlic, onion, and the cumin and mustard seed if desired. Sauté until the onion becomes translucent. Reduce the heat if necessary to keep the onion from browning.

Add the curry powder, and continue to cook briefly, stirring, taking care not to scorch the curry.

Stir in the tomato paste until thoroughly blended. Gradually stir in the liquid reserved from the garbanzos until the sauce is smooth.

Stir in the water. (If you reduced the heat earlier, turn it back up to medium high.) Add the cauliflower florets, potato chunks, and drained garbanzos. When the curry begins to boil, reduce the heat to low.

Some optional additions at this point are carrot, eggplant, or zucchini chunks, mushrooms, or fresh or frozen green beans.

Cook over low heat for at least 2 hours. The longer the cooking time (within reason; the vegetables should not disintegrate), the more integrated the flavor. In view of this long cooking time, it is a good idea to make the cauliflower florets and the potato chunks on the large side.

At the end of the cooking time, gently stir in the hardboiled eggs.

When ready to serve add cayenne pepper to taste, if desired.

Serve with rice (brown Basmati is especially delicious), a good mango chutney, and raita (a mixture of yogurt, finely shredded cucumber, and dried, crumbled mint leaves).

Hardboiled eggs, 1 or 2 per person, shelled but left whole
Cayenne pepper (optional)

Polenta Timbales with Spicy Eggplant Sauce

JEANNE LEMLIN

*Jeanne Lemlin has been a cooking teacher and is a cookbook author.
Her* Vegetarian Pleasures *and* Quick Vegetarian Pleasures *are filled with recipes
for inventive and healthy fare. These timbales are a good example: they are
so substantial that they need only a salad on the side to make a complete meal. They are
also perfect for entertaining—they look striking, and can be prepared well in advance.*

SERVES 4

Timbales:
2-1/4 cups lowfat milk
2-1/4 cups water
1-1/4 cup cornmeal
1/4 cup sour cream
1/4 cup grated
    Parmesan cheese
1/4 teaspoon salt
1/8 teaspoon nutmeg
Freshly ground pepper
1 cup (4 ounces) finely
    diced Italian Fontina
8 thin 1-inch-square
    slices of Italian
    Fontina

To prepare the timbales:
Have ready 8 custard cups or ramekins. Arrange all of the ingredients in front of you before you begin cooking. Bring the milk and water to a boil in a medium-size heavy-bottomed saucepan. Reduce the heat to low, then drizzle in the cornmeal, whisking all the while with a wire whisk. Whisk constantly for about 5 minutes, until the polenta pulls away from the sides of the pan.

Remove from the heat and whisk in the sour cream, Parmesan cheese, salt, nutmeg, and pepper to taste. Stir in the cubes of Fontina just until the cubes are evenly distributed but not melted. Quickly spoon the mixture into the custard cups, then smooth the tops of the timbales with the back of a spoon, or overfill them and scrape off the excess with a knife. Set aside for 15 minutes.

The timbales may be prepared in advance to this point, covered, and refrigerated for up to 24 hours.

Preheat the oven to 400°.

To make the spicy eggplant sauce:
In a large skillet, heat 2 tablespoons of the olive oil over medium heat until hot but not smoking. Add half of the eggplant; cook until almost tender, tossing frequently. Do not add more oil: just keep tossing if the eggplant begins to stick. Remove onto a platter. Add 2 more tablespoons of oil to the skillet; repeat with the remaining eggplant.

In the remaining tablespoon of oil, cook the garlic and red pepper flakes, tossing frequently, until the garlic is golden. Add the remaining ingredients, except the parsley, and bring to a boil. Add the eggplant and cook for 7 to 10 minutes until tender and the sauce has thickened. If the sauce is too thick before the eggplant is done, thin with a little of the reserved tomato liquid. Keep warm over low heat while you bake the timbales.

To bake the timbales:
Generously butter a large, shallow broilerproof baking dish. Invert the timbales into the dish. Top each timbale with a slice of Fontina. Bake at 400° for 15 minutes, then broil for 3 minutes, or until the cheese is bubbly. Remove from the oven, and spread the cheese more evenly over the timbales. Broil for 2 more minutes or until golden.

If the sauce has thickened, add a few more tablespoons of the reserved tomato liquid. Stir in the minced parsley. Serve 2 timbales per person with the eggplant sauce surrounding them.

Spicy eggplant sauce:
5 tablespoons olive oil
1 medium to large (1-1/4 to 1-1/2 pound) eggplant, peeled, cut into 1/2-inch dice
4 cloves garlic, minced
1/4 teaspoon dried red pepper flakes
35-ounce can imported plum tomatoes, coarsely chopped and drained (reserve liquid)
1 tablespoon tomato paste
2 teaspoons red wine vinegar
1/2 teaspoon salt
Liberal seasoning of freshly ground pepper
1-1/2 tablespoon minced fresh parsley

ENTRÉES

85

Oven-Roasted Eggplant with Tomato Feta Coulis

BERKSHIRE PLACE GOURMET FOODS

*Chef Dayne Edwin Kelly developed this recipe during her years as a cook
on a private yacht. "We were at sea for two weeks," she recalls, "and running out
of supplies. We arrived in Exuna, a small island two days south of the Bahamas,
and the only produce I could find for dinner was eggplant and tomatoes."
At Berkshire Place, breakfast, lunch, and some dinners are served,
and there's takeout, too. A full catering service is also available.*

SERVES 4

1 medium eggplant, cut
    into 1/2-inch slices
Olive oil for brushing
    on the eggplant

Tomato feta coulis:
1/2 cup extra virgin
    olive oil
3 large tomatoes
2 cloves garlic, chopped
1/2 cup dry white wine
1 tablespoon balsamic
    vinegar
1 sprig of fresh
    rosemary
1 teaspoon oregano
4 ounces feta cheese
Salt and pepper
4 sprigs of fresh
    rosemary for garnish

Preheat the oven to 350°.

Arrange the sliced eggplant on a baking sheet and brush with olive oil. Bake for 20 minutes. Distribute the slices among four plates.

To make the tomato feta coulis:
Into a large pan, put 1/3 cup of the olive oil and sauté the tomato and garlic over medium-high heat for 5 minutes. Add the white wine and sauté for 2 minutes longer. Add the balsamic vinegar, rosemary, oregano, feta cheese, and salt and pepper, and cook for 2 more minutes.

Remove from the heat and spoon the tomato feta coulis over the roasted eggplant. Garnish with the rosemary sprigs and drizzle the remaining olive oil on the rim of the plate.

Snack à la Arlo

ARLO GUTHRIE

*Musician Arlo Guthrie has been identified with the Berkshires
ever since the movie* Alice's Restaurant. *He recently purchased "Alice's Church"
as home to the Guthrie Center, a foundation whose mission ranges from delivering
meals to AIDS patients to music programs for needy kids.*

"Preheat the TV to the desired channel.

"Spread gobs of the first three ingredients between pieces of the fourth one.

"Pour the milk into a glass. Put the stuff on a paper plate and pour Fritos over the whole thing.

"Sit back in front of the tube. Munch until it's gone."

SERVES lots

1 jar of super crunch
  peanut butter
1 jar of AG's home-
  made black raspberry
  jam (substitutes
  available anywhere)
1 jar of Hellman's Real
  Mayonnaise
1 loaf of nutritionally
  useless white bread
1 big glass of real milk
  (no lowfat or 2% fake
  stuff)
Lots of Fritos
1 good TV show (like
  reruns of Star Trek)

SIDE DISHES

Black Pepper Pasta with Snow Peas & Red Peppers with Spicy Oriental Sauce

THE WRIGHT PASTA COMPANY

This quick and elegant dish can be hotter and spicier, if desired; the black pepper pasta itself also adds some heat. Additional hot sesame oil could be served with the pasta to suit individual tastes. Black pepper pasta can, of course, be purchased from the Wright Pasta Company.

SERVES 4 to 6

1 pound black pepper pasta
4 quarts water
Salt (optional)
1 teaspoon olive oil or sesame oil
2 red bell peppers, julienned
1 small onion, julienned
1-1/2 cup snow peas, julienned

Spicy oriental sauce:
1/4 cup ginger-flavored soy sauce
1/8 cup soy sauce
1/8 cup sesame oil
Hot sesame oil (optional)

Bring the water to a boil, salt if desired, and add the pasta. When the water returns to the boil, check the pasta for doneness. Cook only until al dente. Cool the pasta with cold water, drain, and coat immediately with the 1 teaspoon oil to keep the pasta from sticking together.

Toss in the red peppers, onion, and snow peas. Set aside.

To make the spicy oriental sauce:
In a separate bowl, combine the ingredients. Mix well.

To serve, toss the sauce with the pasta and vegetables. Serve at room temperature.

Samara's Sesame Noodle Sauce

DANIEL KLEIN

"When I was courting my wife-to-be, Freke, in Amsterdam some seventeen years ago, I found myself spending a lot of time in Indonesian restaurants waiting for her to come home from work. These restaurants provide by far the most interesting and inexpensive food in Holland. Indonesian food appeals to me because, like Szechuan cuisine, it is both sweet and piquant. Two ingredients are indispensable for Indonesian cooking, even for the ersatz Indonesian meals I cook up in my Berkshire kitchen: sambal, a hot red pepper relish; and ketjap, a sweet soy sauce whose name gave rise to the word 'ketchup.' Samara's Sesame Noodle Sauce, a concoction of my own, is named after our daughter."

SERVES 6

**Samara's
  sesame sauce:**
1 cup tahini
1/3 cup water
1/3 cup white vinegar
1/3 cup ketjap (not
  ketchup; see above)
2 cloves garlic
2 tablespoons molasses
1 tablespoon tamarind
  syrup (optional)

1 pound pasta
1/2 cup chopped
  scallions or chives for
  garnish

To make Samara's sesame sauce:
Combine the sauce ingredients in a food processor, adding them in the order listed. Mix until smooth.

To prepare the pasta:
Cook the pasta according to the package directions, a bit past al dente, then rinse with cold water to stop the cooking process. Mix in the sesame sauce and garnish with the scallions or chives.

Pasta Gorgonzola Miraculous

THE SPRINGS RESTAURANT

*Chef Edmond Grosso tells this story about the origin of this recipe's name.
"Some time ago an elderly woman using two crutches entered the Springs for lunch.
She and her party ate on the day this dish was introduced. Two hours later, when
I went back into the dining room, she had departed, but her two crutches still rested
against the back of her chair. So we christened the recipe after her:
Pasta Gorgonzola Miraculous."*

To make the Gorgonzola sauce:
In a saucepan, dissolve the beef bouillon cube in the hot water. Add the rest of the ingredients and boil, while stirring, until the onions are cooked through.

To prepare the pasta:
Boil the rotelle according to the package directions and drain thoroughly.

Combine the pasta and the sauce and add ground pepper to taste. Serve with grated cheese on the side.

SERVES 6

Gorgonzola sauce:
1 beef bouillon cube
2 cups hot water
1 onion, chopped
1 cup skim milk
3 tablespoons corn oil
2 tablespoons vodka
1/4 cup Triple Sec or
    Cointreau
2 thin slices ham,
    chopped
3 ounces Gorgonzola
    cheese, crumbled
8 ounces frozen
    chopped spinach
3 ounces lowfat ricotta
    cheese

Pasta:
1 pound rotelle
Freshly ground pepper
Grated cheese on the
    side

Fresh Tomato Basil Spaghetti

LAUREN SMITH

"I wait all year for tomato season and when it comes this dish is the all-time favorite. Cooking, peeling, and even seeding is not necessary. Really simple, really delicious. I like to get the tomatoes, garlic, and herbs at the Great Barrington Farmers' Market — every Saturday during the summer you can buy locally grown produce right from the farmer."

SERVES 4

6 large, ripe tomatoes, cut into 1-inch cubes

3/4 cup julienned fresh basil

3/4 cup olive oil

2 cloves of fresh garlic, chopped

1/4 cup diced red onion

Pasta for four

Salt and pepper

2 tablespoons chopped fresh parsley

Freshly grated Parmesan cheese

Toss the first five ingredients in a bowl. Let stand at room temperature for 1 to 2 hours.

Cook the pasta al dente. Spoon the sauce over the pasta, and sprinkle generously with salt and pepper and the parsley. Top with the Parmesan cheese.

94

Marinara Sauce

CANYON RANCH IN THE BERKSHIRES

Marinara sauce is central to hearty Italian cooking, but it has been much maligned because the traditional versions are full of sodium and often high in calories. This good-for-you version has all the flavor punch with none of the drawbacks.

In a large saucepan, sauté the onion and garlic in the stock with the crushed herbs, bay leaf, and black pepper until the onions are tender. Add the mushrooms if desired and cook for 5 minutes.

Stir in the tomato sauce and tomato purée. Cover and simmer over low heat for 1 hour.

SERVES 6

1 cup chopped onions
1 tablespoon minced
   garlic
1/2 cup vegetable stock
1 teaspoon finely
   chopped fresh
   oregano
3/4 teaspoon finely
   chopped fresh basil
1 bay leaf
1/2 teaspoon ground
   black pepper
2 cups sliced fresh
   mushrooms
   (optional)
3 cups canned
   low-sodium tomato
   sauce
2 cups canned
   low-sodium tomato
   purée

SIDE DISHES

Triple Cheese Ravioli

TRUFFLES & SUCH

*Preparing homemade ravioli is a labor of love, and with a sumptuous filling,
such as this one developed by Truffles & Such, the results are worth it.
A batch of these in the freezer is like having a pot of gold stashed away.*

MAKES 50 ravioli

Pasta:
2 cups flour
4 eggs

Cheese filling:
1 cup ricotta cheese
1/2 cup grated
   provolone cheese
1 cup crumbled blue
   cheese
1/3 cup toasted pine
   nuts
2 tablespoons minced
   parsley
3 tablespoons chopped
   fresh basil
3 tablespoons chopped
   black olives
2 scallions, chopped
2 eggs
3/4 teaspoon freshly
   ground black pepper

Sauce to serve over the
   ravioli, such as
   roasted red pepper
   and tomato sauce or
   a chunky basil pesto

To make the pasta:
Place the flour and the eggs into a food processor all at once and mix with a steel blade until a ball forms. Remove the dough and let it rest for 20 minutes.

To make the cheese filling:
Place the ingredients into a large bowl and mix well.

To assemble the ravioli:
Roll the dough out with a pasta machine, taking care not to use too much flour or the ravioli will not seal properly. Use a ravioli cutter or a pizza cutter to make the ravioli squares. Top each ravioli square with 2 teaspoons of the cheese filling and place another square over the top. Seal the edges, moistening them if necessary to get a proper seal.

Refrigerate in a single layer, or freeze.

To serve, cook the ravioli in rapidly boiling water for 12 to 15 minutes. Top with sauce.

Wild Rice Cakes

JOHN ANDREW'S RESTAURANT

The elegant John Andrew's, located just outside South Egremont, serves its unique version of American cuisine: fresh ingredients, a blending of international cuisines, and a sure hand with seasonings. These wild rice cakes are great with roasted or grilled meats.

Rinse the wild rice, drain, and place it into a small saucepan with the water, thyme, bay leaves, salt, and pepper. Cover and bring to a boil; lower the heat and simmer for 1 hour until the rice is tender but not disintegrated.

Meanwhile, prepare the batter by placing the flour into a mixing bowl and making a well in the center. Pour in the milk and egg, and whip to combine. Reserve.

When the rice is tender, add the carrot, onion, celery, and garlic; cover again and steam until the vegetables are tender but crisp. Cool and fold into the batter.

Heat a nonstick skillet, and add some of the butter or peanut oil. Measure 1/4 cup of wild-rice batter and cook for 1 to 2 minutes until the pancake is browned and cooked through. Keep warm and make the rest of the cakes, adding more butter or oil as needed.

MAKES 16 small cakes

1 cup wild rice
2 cups water
4 sprigs of thyme
2 small bay leaves
1 teaspoon salt
1/2 teaspoon freshly
   ground pepper
1 cup diced carrot
3/4 cup diced onion
3/4 cup diced celery
2 small cloves of garlic,
   finely chopped
1 cup flour
3/4 cup milk
1 large egg
2 tablespoons unsalted
   butter or peanut oil

Embree's Mashed Potatoes

EMBREE'S RESTAURANT

*Sometimes a recipe is beyond measurements. These are the mashed potatoes
that will nourish and warm on a cold winter's eve, after a skating party on one
of the frozen lakes. And use real butter: it will satisfy as nothing else can.*

SERVES you
and those you love

Potatoes
Water
Unsalted butter
Milk
Freshly ground pepper
Garlic, puréed in a food
 processor
Finely chopped parsley
 for garnish
Optional toppings: sour
 cream; chopped red
 onion; chopped
 chives

Wash the potatoes thoroughly, leaving the skins on. Cut into cubes, put them into a pot, and cover with water. Bring the water to a boil and simmer for about 25 minutes until the potatoes are soft enough to mash.

Mash with a wooden mallet. Add lots of unsalted butter, a little milk, pepper, and garlic. Taste and then add salt if you think it needs it. Taste and add more garlic and pepper if you wish.

Preheat the oven to 350°.

Put the mashed potatoes into an ovenproof bowl and place it in the oven at 350° for 10 to 15 minutes, until a golden-brown crust forms on the top. Spoon out and garnish with parsley.

Serve with your favorite toppings.

Refried Beans

DOS AMIGOS MEXICAN RESTAURANT

Dos Amigos has developed this recipe over the years, pleasing customers with its consistency and taste. It's a perfect party dish; this recipe makes a large quantity.

Soak the beans overnight in the water.

Place all the ingredients, except the cheese, into a heavy saucepan. If the beans have soaked up all the water, add enough water to cover the beans.

Cook over medium-low heat for 2 to 3 hours until the beans are very soft.

Mash the beans, and serve topped with shredded cheddar cheese if desired.

SERVES 50 as a side dish, or 25 as a main dish

8 cups pinto beans, sorted
16 cups water
1 large onion, quartered
2 tomatoes, cored
Splash of vegetable oil
2 tablespoons granulated garlic
2-1/2 tablespoons salt
1/2 teaspoon black pepper
1/2 tablespoon ground cumin
Shredded cheddar cheese (optional)

SIDE DISHES

VEGETABLES & SALADS

Sautéed Red Cabbage with Walnuts and Chèvre

DAVID EMBLIDGE

"The humble but exotically hued red cabbage rises to new heights when combined with goat cheese and nuts. Locally made goat cheese from Rawson Brook Farm and cabbage fresh from a Berkshire farm yield the best results. After the shredding and chopping are done, this eye-pleasing dish almost cooks itself. A creative juxtaposition of elements and a bright splash of color, this delicious vegetable side dish is excellent with red meat or fowl." A twenty-year Berkshire resident, with forays into Boston, New York, and France, David Emblidge is a writer, editor, and enthusiastic home cook. He founded Berkshire House Publishers in 1985, served as its publisher until 1992, and commissioned this book.

Discard any wilted outer cabbage leaves and cut away the tough stem. Slice the cabbage into 1/4-inch sections, then shred coarsely by hand or with a knife. Discard the heavy pieces from the core.

In a large skillet, briefly heat half the oil. Sauté the garlic for 1 minute. Add the walnuts and toss with the oil and garlic; sauté 3 to 5 minutes, stirring frequently.

Add the shredded cabbage and toss it with the garlic and nuts, adding the remaining oil to coat the cabbage thoroughly. Sauté at medium to high heat for 8 to 10 minutes or until the cabbage is hot yet still al dente. Toss frequently.

Quickly drop dabs of chèvre onto the cabbage, allowing the cheese to melt slightly. Toss gently once more, and serve.

SERVES 4 to 6

1 medium-sized red cabbage, 4 to 6 inches in diameter
2 tablespoons walnut oil or olive oil
4 cloves of garlic, coarsely chopped
1 cup coarsely chopped walnuts
4 ounces plain or garlic-flavored chèvre, or ricotta

Baked Artichokes with Onions & Sweet Peppers

JOHN ANDREW'S RESTAURANT

This elegant dish can be made up to two days ahead and reheated with no loss of flavor. Leftovers can be tossed with pasta the next day to make a great lunch.

SERVES 6

12 small artichokes,
    1-1/2 to 2 ounces
    each
Water
Juice of 2 lemons
1/2 cup extra virgin
    olive oil, divided
2 medium onions,
    thinly sliced
2 red bell peppers,
    seeded and sliced
2 yellow bell peppers,
    seeded and sliced
6 sprigs of thyme
2 small bay leaves
1 teaspoon salt, divided
Freshly ground black
    pepper
Leaves of 6 sprigs of
    Italian parsley for
    garnish

Preheat the oven to 350°.

Prepare the artichokes by removing the top half inch of the leaves (easily done with kitchen scissors) and cutting the artichokes in half. Pick off the tougher outer leaves and place the artichokes into a bowl with water to cover and the lemon juice.

In another bowl, combine the onions, red peppers, yellow peppers, 1/4 cup of the olive oil, the thyme, bay leaves, 1/2 teaspoon of the salt, and black pepper.

Drain the artichokes and toss with the remaining 1/4 cup olive oil, the remaining 1/2 teaspoon salt, and season with additional black pepper.

Place the onion-and-pepper mixture into a shallow enameled or glass baking pan and arrange the artichokes, cut side down, over the top.

Cover with baking paper or wax paper, and then cover tightly with aluminum foil. Bake for 1 hour at 350° or until the artichokes are tender.

Divide among six warm plates and sprinkle with the Italian parsley.

BEST RECIPES OF BERKSHIRE CHEFS

Asparagus, Morels & Shaved Parmesan

JOHN ANDREW'S RESTAURANT

When asparagus and morels are available in the spring, this combination is rewarding and rejuvenating. However, if the urge to have this dish strikes out of season, all is not lost: asparagus can usually be found year round, and dried morels can be substituted for fresh.

Trim the asparagus spears and blanch them by dipping into boiling water for 1 minute. Remove and drain.

Trim the stems from the morels, check for dirt, and wipe clean if needed, but do not rinse with water. Cut the morels in halves or quarters, depending on their size.

To make the marinade:
Combine the ingredients. Add the morels and marinate for 30 minutes.

To make the vinaigrette:
Combine the ingredients, seasoning to taste with the salt and pepper.

To prepare the morels:
Heat a sauté pan until very hot (close to smoking point), and saute the morels for 1 minute.

On a chilled plate, arrange the asparagus and morels, sprinkle with the Parmesan, lemon zest, and pepper. Drizzle with the vinaigrette.

SERVES 4

24 asparagus spears
8 ounces fresh morels
2 tablespoons shaved
  Parmesan
Zest of 1 lemon
Freshly ground black
  pepper

Marinade:
4 tablespoons olive oil
1 tablespoons chopped
  parsley
1 teaspoon fresh thyme
  leaves
1 shallot, finely diced
Pinch of salt
Freshly ground black
  pepper

Vinaigrette:
4 tablespoons extra
  virgin olive oil
1 shallot, finely diced
1 teaspoon chopped
  garlic
Juice of 1 lemon
Salt
Freshly ground pepper

Perfect Corn on the Cob

TAFT FARMS

Taft Farms' Integrated Pest Management (IPM) program has enabled them to avoid using pesticide sprays on many of their major crops, such as sweet corn, for several years. IPM is a crop management system that controls crop pests by means of natural predators, constant field scouting, and crop rotation. The friendly folks at Taft Farms are glad to explain how their produce is grown safely and organically.

SERVES any number

As many ears of corn as you can fit into your cooking pot
Water

Microwaved corn:
1 to 5 ears of unhusked corn

Husk the corn. Bring a large pot of water to a boil. Drop in the husked ears of corn and bring the pot to a boil again.

Set the timer for no more than 2 to 3 minutes. (There is no need to cook the cob.) Boil only until the kernels begin to change color.

Serve immediately.

Microwaved corn:
Place the corn, in its husk, in a shallow casserole in the microwave. Cover.

Microwave for 3 to 4 minutes per ear, with power level set to high.

After half the cooking time, rearrange the ears for even cooking.

Sister Mary's Zesty Carrots

HANCOCK SHAKER VILLAGE

A recipe from the manuscripts of the Hancock Shakers (1790-1960), this delicious side dish has been featured at the Hancock Shaker Village Candlelight Shaker Dinners. The evening program recreates a four-course Shaker meal served in the Believers' Dining Room, with authentic recipes prepared by Crosby's Catering. The Shakers used the fresh produce from their gardens and planned their meals to "create enjoyment, joy, and satisfaction to those partaking of them."

Preheat the oven to 375°.

Clean and cut the carrots into thin strips. Cook until tender in salted water. Drain the carrots and place them into a 6" x 10" baking dish.

Mix together the onion, horseradish, mayonnaise, salt, pepper, and water. Pour this over the carrots. Sprinkle the buttered breadcrumbs over the top.

Bake at 375° for about 15 minutes.

SERVES 4 to 6

6 carrots
Salt
Water to cover
2 tablespoons grated onion
2 tablespoons horseradish
1/2 cup mayonnaise
1 teaspoon salt
1/4 teaspoon pepper
1/4 cup water
1/4 cup buttered bread crumbs

Warm Green Salad with Chicken

GEORGEANNE ROUSSEAU

"This salad is ideal for showing off the different varieties of salad greens growing in your garden. It makes a lovely offering for a summer luncheon or fancy buffet."

SERVES 8

Salad:

1/2 teaspoon finely minced garlic

Salt and freshly ground pepper

1 tablespoon Dijon mustard

5 teaspoons red wine vinegar

5 tablespoons walnut or light olive oil

16 cups loosely packed mixed greens

2 teaspoons each chopped fresh tarragon, basil, and chervil

1 teaspoon chopped fresh parsley

2 teaspoons oil

1 chicken liver, cut into 1/2-inch cubes (optional)

1/4 cup chopped scallions

2 teaspoons red wine vinegar

To make the salad:

Combine the garlic, salt and pepper, mustard, and the 5 teaspoons red wine vinegar in a large salad bowl. Using a wire whisk, gradually add the 5 tablespoons walnut oil until all is mixed in.

Add the greens (try oakleaf, redleaf, little gem, romaine, curly endive, cress, mâche, simpson, or other available varieties) and the fresh herbs, but do not toss at this point.

Heat the 2 teaspoons oil in a small skillet and when it is very hot, almost smoking, add the chicken liver if desired. Cook quickly, tossing and stirring for 30 seconds, and then add the scallions and the 2 teaspoons red wine vinegar. Stir quickly over high heat and pour over the salad greens. Toss well to coat the leaves with the dressing at the bottom of the bowl.

Spoon the dressed greens onto eight individual plates.

To prepare the chicken:

Lightly pound the chicken pieces with a flat mallet, and cut them into uniform, attractive pieces. Slice them into thin, bias-cut strips and arrange these neatly on a sheet of wax paper. Further thin the strips by pounding them lightly, taking care to keep the pieces whole.

Heat the 2 teaspoons oil in a large skillet and add the chicken breast pieces. Cook for about 30 seconds on one side; turn and cook for 30 seconds on the other. Immediately before serving, season the chicken strips with salt and pepper. Arrange equal amounts of the chicken over each serving of salad greens.

To the skillet in which the chicken breast pieces were cooked, over high heat, add the 2 teaspoons red wine vinegar, stir and scrape up any chicken bits, and pour the boiling vinegar over the salad. Serve at once.

Chicken:

2 pounds boneless, skinless chicken breasts

2 teaspoons oil

Salt and freshly ground pepper

2 teaspoons red wine vinegar

Salad of Seared Shrimp & Radicchio

BLANTYRE

Blantyre is today what it was designed to be—the very finest expression of domestic elegance and comfort. Lovingly restored to its original turn-of-the-century Tudor splendor by Jane and Jack Fitzpatrick, proprietors of the famed Red Lion Inn, Blantyre is the Berkshires' only Relais et Chateaux member. Built by businessman Robert Paterson, Blantyre is a replica of his wife's ancestral home in the Scottish village of Blantyre, east of Glasgow.

SERVES 4

1-1/2 pounds radicchio
1/2 pound large shrimp
1 tablespoon sherry
  vinegar
3 tablespoons hazelnut
  oil
2 tablespoons olive oil
Salt and pepper
1 tablespoon dark soy
  sauce
1 tablespoon
  Worcestershire sauce

Warm four individual plates.

Clean and wash the radicchio. Dry the leaves gently between two towels.

Peel and devein the shrimp and cut them into half-inch chunks.

Make a vinaigrette with the sherry vinegar and hazelnut oil. Pour the vinaigrette over the radicchio in a bowl and toss.

Sauté the chunks of shrimp in a very hot pan with the olive oil and the salt and pepper.

Deglaze the pan, first with the soy sauce, then with the Worcestershire sauce. Pour over the salad immediately.

Serve at once on the warmed plates.

Shrimp Salad with Citrus Sections & Celery Poppy Dressing

THE RED LION INN

Ever since the days of stagecoach travel, the Red Lion Inn has been serving up fine fare and warm hospitality to travelers and residents. Whether traditional New England favorites or delicious contemporary dishes, the Red Lion is justly famous for its cuisine, and for its dining settings—the elegant main dining room, the cozy Widow Bingham's Tavern, the downstairs Lion's Den pub, and, in the summer, the flower-bedecked courtyard and the spacious front porch.

SERVES 4

Skin and seed the grapefruit and orange, and separate them into sections, being careful to remove all membranes.

Peel the red onion and slice it very thin, separating into rings.

To make the celery poppy dressing:
In a small bowl or a jar with a cover, combine the sugar, dry mustard, salt, and white pepper. Add the vinegar and the celery seed and poppy seed. Mix or shake well; add the oil and mix well. Finish to taste with salt and pepper.

To assemble the salad, combine the citrus sections and the shrimp. Toss lightly with 1/2 cup of dressing. Marinate for 10 minutes, and keep chilled.

Arrange the avocado on chilled salad plates and fill with the fruit and shrimp mixture. Top each with 4 onion rings, drizzle with 1 tablespoon of dressing, and garnish with a lime wedge. Serve the remaining dressing on the side.

1 large pink grapefruit
1 large navel orange
1 small red onion
12 cooked and cleaned cocktail shrimp
2 large ripe avocados, halved, pitted, and peeled
Lime wedges for garnish

Celery poppy dressing:
1/4 cup sugar
2 teaspoons dry mustard
1/4 teaspoon salt
1/8 teaspoon white pepper
1/2 cup white vinegar
2 teaspoons celery seed
1-1/2 teaspoon poppy seed
2 cups corn oil

Caesar Salad

STEVEN HAAS

Architect Steven Haas has made the Berkshires his home for the last four years. His wife, Roberta, is Director of Performing Arts at the Berkshire Museum. Steven specializes in the design of high-quality residences, and was recently honored by Architectural Digest *as one of the world's foremost architects.*

SERVES 4

1 head of romaine
   lettuce
1/2 McIntosh apple
2 thin slices of red
   onion or Vidalia
   onion

Caesar dressing:
8 flat anchovy fillets,
   drained and finely
   chopped
4 medium cloves of
   garlic, minced
3 tablespoons extra
   virgin olive oil
3 tablespoons canola oil
1-1/2 tablespoon
   balsamic vinegar
1 tablespoon Dijon
   mustard
Juice of 1/2 lemon
1 tablespoon
   mayonnaise
1/2 teaspoon
   Worcestershire sauce
1/3 cup freshly
   shredded Parmesan
Freshly ground pepper

Remove the tough outer leaves from the lettuce, separate the remaining leaves, wash, spin dry, and break the leaves in half. Set aside.

Cut the apple into small wedges. Separate the onion slices into rings. Set aside.

To make the Caesar dressing:
In a salad bowl, mix together the anchovies and the minced garlic to make a paste. Add the rest of the dressing ingredients and mix well.

Just before serving, add the lettuce, apple, and onion rings. Mix well with the dressing.

Just before serving, top with the warm croutons.

To make the sourdough croutons:
Combine the butter and garlic. Butter both sides of the bread. Cut into large croutons. Pan-fry them right before serving until crisp on all sides.

Sourdough croutons:
2 tablespoons butter
1 teaspoon minced garlic
2 slices of sourdough bread

Endive Salad

FREDI HUNGATE

"The center core of the endive tends to be very bitter but if you slice off the lower end, pull off the leaves that come off easily, slice again and again pull off the outer leaves, you can easily get to the core and remove it." Fredi brought this recipe back from the Netherlands where she lived for many years. Andijvie sla, as it is called there, is a popular lunch dish. The word sla, Dutch for salad, is the source of the American word slaw.

SERVES 4

4 Belgian endives
2 hardboiled eggs
1 tablespoon minced
　onion
1/4 cup mayonnaise
Oil
Vinegar
Salt and pepper

Slice the endives thinly.

Chop the hardboiled eggs.

Mix together the endives, eggs, onion, and mayonnaise.

Thin out to the desired consistency with a little bit of oil and vinegar. Add salt and pepper to taste.

Chilled Asparagus in Sesame Sauce

CASTLE STREET CAFÉ

Chef Michael Ballon of the Castle Street Café takes pride in using the best locally grown or produced ingredients in preparing its fine fare. This café next door to the historic Mahaiwe Theatre welcomes diners and the after-the-movie coffee-and-dessert folks with friendliness and fresh flowers on the table.

Blanch the asparagus spears in boiling water for 30 seconds, then plunge them into ice water to stop the cooking process. Drain well.

Toast the sesame seeds for 2 to 3 minutes in a skillet without any oil, until they are lightly browned.

To make the sesame sauce:
In a small bowl, combine the egg yolk, mustard, and vinegar, and while whisking slowly add the oils. Be sure to mix well. Then whisk in the soy sauce and honey.

Spoon the sauce over the bottom of the plate, fan the asparagus on top, and sprinkle with the toasted sesame seeds.

SERVES 4 to 6

1-1/2 pound thin
   asparagus spears
2 tablespoons sesame
   seeds

Sesame sauce:
1 egg yolk
1 tablespoon Pommery
   mustard
2 tablespoons red wine
   vinegar
1/2 cup soybean oil
6 tablespoons toasted
   sesame oil
1 tablespoon soy sauce
1 tablespoon honey

Raspberry Vinaigrette

COBBLE CAFÉ

A salad dressing that distills the flavors of summer, whatever the season.
The rosy color of the vinaigrette looks particularly appealing on a bed of mixed greens.
Additional chopped walnuts sprinkled on top will accentuate the walnut flavor.

SERVES 4 to 8

1 cup frozen
  raspberries, thawed
1 cup raspberry vinegar
2 cups corn oil
1/4 cup walnut oil
  (optional)
4 to 5 ounces chopped
  walnuts
Chopped walnuts for
  garnish (optional)

Place half of the thawed raspberries and the raspberry vinegar into a blender container. Blend for 5 seconds.

With the blender running slowly, add the corn oil, and then the walnut oil if desired.

Turn off the blender. Add the remaining raspberries and the walnuts. Blend for 1 second.

Serve over your favorite salad. Garnish with additional chopped walnuts if desired.

116

PICNIC FARE
& OUTDOOR
FOOD

EEB 4-93

Grilled Chicken with Many-Mustards Sauce

TRUFFLES & SUCH

Many recipes for the grill, including this one, are ideal for summer fare since the actual cooking is not particularly complicated. The sauce can be made ahead of time and the grilling can be a leisurely affair, long cool drink in hand. Chef Irene Maston recommends roast potatoes on the side.

To make the many mustards sauce:
Combine the ingredients in a small bowl.

To grill the chicken:
Preheat the grill and start grilling the chicken breasts. When the chicken is half cooked on the second side, spread with the sauce and finish cooking.

Grill the apples for 3 minutes on each side, and serve them with the chicken.

SERVES 6

Many mustards sauce:
1/4 cup Dijon mustard
2 tablespoons
   peppercorn mustard
2 tablespoons
   horseradish mustard
2 teaspoons green
   peppercorns
1/2 cup sour cream
1 tablespoon dry
   vermouth

Chicken:
6 boneless, skinless
   chicken breasts,
   6 ounces each
3 apples, cut in wedges

Chicken Satay

DANIEL KLEIN

*"Chicken Satay is a fast-food snack in Holland. I'm convinced someone could make
a million on it in the United States. I can see it now: Indonesian Taco Bells
dotting our highways. You read it first here in the Berkshires."
Daniel Klein is a novelist, journalist, and food reviewer.*

SERVES 4

3 pair of boneless,
  skinless chicken
  breasts

Marinade:
1/4 cup ketjap*
1/4 cup lemon juice
2 tablespoons vodka

Satay sauce:
1 onion, finely chopped
2 cloves garlic, crushed
2 tablespoons sambal*
1 tablespoon trasi
  (shrimp paste;
  optional)
1 tablespoon brown
  sugar
2 tablespoons
  margarine
12-ounce jar peanut
  butter
2 cups coconut milk
2 tablespoons ketjap
1 tablespoon tamarind
  syrup (optional)
Grated rind and juice of
  1 lime
*See page 92.

Cut the chicken into 1-inch cubes.

To marinate the chicken:
Mix the marinade ingredients, toss with
the chicken, and set aside for 1 hour.

To make the satay sauce:
With a mortar and pestle, mash the
onion, garlic, sambal, trasi if desired,
and the brown sugar to form a paste.

Melt the margarine in a large skillet and
add the paste. Cook for 2 to 3 minutes
over low heat.

Add the peanut butter and stir to blend.
Gradually add the coconut milk, slowly
raising the heat and blending until the
sauce thickens. Add the ketjap, and the
tamarind syrup if desired.

Remove from the heat. Add the grated
rind and the juice of the lime.

Thread the marinated chicken onto
skewers and grill or barbecue the
chicken.

Place the skewers on plates and top
generously with the satay sauce. Serve
with rice.

Honey Mustard Shrimp

CHEZ VOUS CATERERS

*These shrimp are excellent as an appetizer or as a cold first course
on a hot summer's night. The sauce is pungent, sweet, and hot all at the same time.
The mustard oil used in this recipe is available in Chinese specialty shops.
Chez Vous has been catering elegant foods since 1982.*

Peel and devein the shrimp.

To marinate the shrimp:
Combine the marinade ingredients and add the shrimp. Refrigerate for 24 hours.

To poach the shrimp:
Drain the shrimp and discard the marinade. Bring a large pot of water to a boil, reduce to a simmer, and poach the shrimp in a basket just until they curl and turn pink.

To make the dipping sauce:
Combine the ingredients in a food processor and serve with the shrimp.

SERVES 8

40 shrimp

Marinade:
1/2 cup unsalted butter
1/2 cup Dijon mustard
1/2 cup honey
1 teaspoon mustard oil
1/2 cup white wine
1 teaspoon chopped
   chives

Dipping sauce:
1/2 cup unsalted butter
1/2 cup honey
1/2 cup Dijon mustard
1 teaspoon mustard oil
1 teaspoon chopped
   chives
Dash of white pepper

Grilled Tofu Kebabs

EMBREE'S RESTAURANT

Joan Embree suggests serving this dish with black beans and rice with saffron and scallions. To keep the chunks of food from slipping on the skewer, use two skewers for each kebab: that makes it much easier to handle, especially when you're turning the kebabs on the grill.

SERVES 8

Marinade:
1/2 cup olive oil
2 tablespoons sesame
    oil
1/4 cup white wine
1/4 cup balsamic
    vinegar
Juice of 2 lemons
2 tablespoons tamari
1 clove of garlic,
    crushed
Pinch of basil
Pinch of thyme

Kebabs:
1 block of firm tofu
2 tomatoes
1 red bell pepper
1 green bell pepper
1 yellow bell pepper
1 medium zucchini
1 red onion
16 large mushroom
    caps

1 lemon, sliced, for
    garnish

To make the marinade:
In a very large bowl, whisk together the ingredients.

To marinate the kebabs:
Cut the tofu and the vegetables, except the mushroom caps, into large chunks. Add the tofu and all the vegetables to the marinade and mix carefully with your hands. Marinate for 1 hour.

To grill the kebabs:
Arrange the chunks randomly on skewers. Grill on an outdoor grill until done. Garnish with the lemon slices.

Baked Mushroom Loaf

RAWSON BROOK FARM

*This dish would make a delicious light supper after a hot summer's day, perhaps
as a picnic on the lawn of The Mount before a performance by Shakespeare & Company.
Some crusty bread from a local bakery, fresh produce from a farm stand,
"a bottle of wine and thou" complete the picture.*

Preheat the oven to 400°.

Chop the mushrooms and sauté them in the olive oil. Add the remaining ingredients. Form into a 2-inch thick log.

Bake on a rimmed cookie sheet at 400° for 30 minutes or until golden brown.

Serve warm or cooled.

SERVES 4

2 tablespoons extra
  virgin olive oil
8 to 10 mushrooms
8 ounces Monterey
  Chèvre, any variety
1 cup flour
1 cup breadcrumbs
1 egg

Panzanella

EMBREE'S RESTAURANT

"This bread salad from Tuscany is a wonderful way to use slightly stale bread. It satisfies that desire to dip one's bread into the leftover vinaigrette in the bottom of the salad bowl," explains Joan Embree. It is also an elegant way to combine a sandwich and a salad and to enjoy the best of the fresh local vegetables at the height of summer. It would be a delightful lunch for a picnic on the Tanglewood lawn.

SERVES 8

Vinaigrette:
1/2 cup olive oil
1/8 cup balsamic vinegar
Juice of 2 lemons
5 fresh basil leaves
4 to 6 cloves of elephant garlic
Freshly ground black pepper

12 slices high-quality bread, thinly sliced, crusts cut off
3 large, juicy tomatoes, thinly sliced
1 cucumber, thinly sliced
2 red bell peppers, thinly sliced
1 large red onion, finely chopped
Small jar of capers
Parmesan
Finely chopped parsley
Green olives for garnish

To make the vinaigrette:
In a small bowl, whisk together the olive oil and vinegar. Add the lemon juice. Cut the basil leaves into very small pieces and mix in. Put the garlic cloves into a food processor and blend until liquefied, or mash them well with a fork. Add to the oil mixture. Add freshly ground black pepper to taste.

To assemble the panzanella:
Pour a little vinaigrette into a shallow serving dish to cover the bottom. Place 4 slices of bread into the dish, then add layers of half of the tomatoes, cucumber, and onion, some capers, and some of the vinaigrette. Add another layer of 4 slices of bread and another layer of vegetables. Top with a final layer of 4 slices of bread.

Pour the remaining vinaigrette over the bread. Sprinkle with Parmesan and chopped parsley, and garnish with olives.

Cut into squares to serve.

Appalachian Trail Couscous

MIRIAM JACOBS

Ideal for Berkshire hiking trips, this couscous takes only 20 minutes to prepare.
All that's needed to complete this backpackable lunch are granola bars and water.
A vegetarian dish such as this one is a good choice for a day hike:
its complex carbohydrates will give you energy, whereas animal protein
can be hard to digest and can make you feel sluggish.

Place a 2-quart plastic container into the freezer.

Place the water into a pan and turn the heat on high. While the water is coming to a boil, cut the fresh corn off the ears and put it into the water. (If you are using frozen corn, add it to the water now. If you are using canned corn, add it later with the cut-up vegetables.) Add the spices and raisins. When the water boils, stir in the couscous, cover, and turn off the heat.

After 10 minutes, fluff up the couscous, letting the steam escape. Put the couscous into the frozen plastic container and place the closed container into the refrigerator.

Mix the remaining ingredients with the couscous. Adjust the seasonings, adding more vinaigrette to taste, and refrigerate until ready to use.

To make Sarah's vinaigrette:
Place the ingredients into a blender container, and whirl for 30 seconds.

SERVES 4 *hungry hikers*

1-1/2 cup water
2 fresh ears of corn, or 1 cup canned or frozen corn
1/2 teaspoon cumin
1/4 teaspoon each turmeric, ginger, coriander, and cardamom
1/4 cup raisins
1 cup couscous
2 celery stalks, diced
1 apple, diced
1 red pepper, diced
1 cup fresh shelled peas
1/4 cup slivered almonds
1/4 cup chopped parsley
1/2 cup Sarah's mustard vinaigrette

Sarah's vinaigrette:
1/2 cup olive oil
1/4 cup cider vinegar
1/4 cup Dijon mustard
1 clove of garlic

Windflower Inn Brownies

WINDFLOWER INN

*Brownies are an American invention and, like chocolate chip cookies,
are virtually unknown in the rest of the world. When melting the chocolate,
put the butter into the pan first and add the chocolate after some of the butter
has melted: that way the chocolate will not stick to the bottom and scorch.*

MAKES a big batch

8 ounces unsweetened
  chocolate
1-1/2 cup unsalted
  butter
6 eggs
3 cups sugar
3 teaspoons vanilla
1 teaspoon salt
1-1/2 cup sifted flour
2-1/2 cups chopped
  pecans

Preheat the oven to 350°.

Liberally butter a 12x18-inch baking pan and dust it with flour. Set aside.

In a heavy saucepan over medium low heat, melt together the chocolate and butter, stirring occasionally.

In a separate bowl, whisk the eggs. Add the sugar, vanilla, and salt, and mix well.

Add the melted chocolate mixture to the egg mixture and mix well. Add the flour and stir just until mixed. Add the nuts and stir just to incorporate.

Pour the batter into the prepared baking pan. Bake at 350° for about 25 minutes.

BEST RECIPES OF BERKSHIRE CHEFS

Apricot Almond Granola Bars

LAUREN SMITH

Lauren Smith organizes "A Taste of the Berkshire Hills," an annual event for local food producers and restaurants to showcase their wares. The tasting and sampling take place in Great Barrington on the first Saturday after Labor Day.

Preheat the oven to 350°.

In a saucepan, mix the honey, apricot jam, cinnamon, vegetable oil, almond extract, and salt. Heat the mixture until it is hot and very liquid.

In a separate bowl, mix the rolled oats, sunflower seeds, chopped almonds, and Rice Krispies.

Pour the liquid ingredients over the dry ingredients, and toss until evenly coated. Spread this mixture onto a well-oiled cookie sheet and bake at 350° for 10 minutes until golden.

Remove from the oven and mix the granola with the apricots. Form the granola into a compact cake, 3/4 inch thick, and return to the oven for another 10 minutes or until brown.

Remove from the oven and let cool completely before cutting into bars. If the bars stick to the pan, place it on top of the warm stove for 15 to 20 seconds. That will soften the bottom of the bars so they can easily be removed with a spatula.

SERVES 12

1/4 cup honey
1/2 cup apricot jam
1 tablespoon cinnamon
1 cup vegetable oil
1 tablespoon almond extract
1 teaspoon salt
3 cups rolled oats
1 cup sunflower seeds
1 cup chopped almonds
1-1/2 cup Rice Krispies
1 cup chopped dried apricots

Swedish Hallon Rutor

BERKSHIRE COUNTRY DAY SCHOOL SPRING FAIR PANTRY SHELF

These are favorites at the BCD Spring Fair Pantry Shelf—simple to make,
yet so elegant looking, and the taste is divine.
A perfect summer dessert to take to a potluck dinner.

YIELDS 50 cookies

1 cup butter
1/3 cup sugar
2 cups flour
Raspberry jam
1 small egg or 1 egg
    yolk, beaten

Preheat the oven to 375°.

Butter a baking sheet.

Work the butter, sugar, and flour together until the dough forms a ball, as for a pie crust. Divide the dough in half.

Between two sheets of wax paper, roll out half the dough to about one quarter inch thick and the size of the baking sheet. Place the dough onto the baking sheet. Spread raspberry jam over the dough.

Cut strips of the remaining dough to make a diagonal lattice pattern on the top of the jam. Brush the top with the beaten egg or egg yolk.

Bake at 375° for 10 to 15 minutes or till light brown.

Cut into squares.

Chocolate Chip Cookies

THE BERKSHIRE COFFEE ROASTING COMPANY

This recipe is recommended for dipping into after-dinner coffee, munching (quietly) on the lawn at Tanglewood, late-night snacking with a glass of milk, or tucking away into a backpack for quick energy on a hike.

Preheat the oven to 325°.

In a large bowl, soften the two kinds of butter and whip with an electric mixer. Add the two kinds of sugar and beat until incorporated. Add the vanilla and the eggs, one at a time, beating after each addition.

In another large bowl, sift together the flour, baking soda, and salt.

Add the dry ingredients to the butter mixture, mixing well. Stir in the oats and chocolate chips and mix well.

Scoop the batter (an ice cream scoop works well) onto cookie sheets and flatten with your fingertips.

Bake at 325° for 12 to 15 minutes or until golden brown around the edges.

YIELDS 5-1/2 dozen

2 cups salted butter, at room temperature
1 cup unsalted butter, at room temperature
2 cups light brown sugar, lightly packed
2 cups white sugar
1 tablespoon vanilla
6 eggs
7 cups organic white flour
1 tablespoon baking soda
1 tablespoon sea salt
4 cups rolled oats
5 cups malt-sweetened chocolate chips

Apple Herbal

NAOMI'S HERBS

*Visit Naomi's Herbs to delight the senses. There are teas to soothe a sore throat,
potpourris to scent drawers and rooms, herbs to flavor a soup,
exotic spices to brighten a curry, and dried flowers to decorate your home.
This pretty red Apple Herbal tea also works well iced.*

MAKES 6 pots of tea

1-1/2 tablespoon apple bits or dried apples

2 teaspoons whole cloves

2 teaspoons allspice berries

2 teaspoons cinnamon chips

3 tablespoons chamomile

3 tablespoons lemongrass

1-1/2 tablespoon hibiscus

If you are using dried apples, cut them up into very small pieces with a pair of scissors.

Place the cloves, allspice berries, and cinnamon chips between two pieces of wax paper and crush them with a hammer, or blend for 1 second in a coffee grinder (don't let the mixture become powder). Mix with the remaining ingredients and store in an airtight jar.

To make the tea, fill a kettle with cold water and bring to a boil. Into a 4-cup teapot, place 2 tablespoons of the tea mix, or one heaping tablespoon for weaker tea. Pour boiling water over the tea mix and let steep for 10 minutes. Pour through a strainer and drink hot or cold.

Add honey or fruit juice to taste if desired.

BEST RECIPES OF BERKSHIRE CHEFS

DESSERTS

Flourless Chocolate Mousse Cake

CASTLE STREET CAFÉ

*For success in baking this rich and very special cake, follow the instructions
to the letter. For the imported chocolate (European specifications for the manufacture
of chocolate are different from American), chef Michael Ballon recommends either Lindt
or Callebaut. Be sure the eggs are warm when they are beaten, and beat for the full
five minutes (so enough air is incorporated to make the cake light). Finally, make sure
the oven doesn't get hotter than 300º. Don't be deterred by these warnings:
the final result will make it all worth while.*

Preheat the oven to 300°.

Butter and flour a 5x9-inch loaf pan, or line it with parchment paper.

In the top of a double boiler, melt the chocolate with the coffee, rum, and vanilla.

Warm the eggs in the top of a double boiler (or in the metal bowl of an electric mixer) until they are warm.

Add the sugar and beat with the electric mixer on high speed for a full 5 minutes until the whole is tripled in volume. Fold in the melted chocolate. Then fold in the whipped cream.

Pour the mixture into the prepared loaf pan. Place the loaf pan into a larger pan of water so that the water comes up 3 inches on the side of the loaf pan. Bake at 300° for 1-1/4 to 1-1/2 hour or until the center is firm.

Chill overnight. Unmold onto a plate and serve at room temperature, with whipped cream on the side.

SERVES 10

Butter and flour, or
  parchment paper, for
  preparing the pan
12 ounces bittersweet
  imported chocolate
1/2 cup strong coffee
1 teaspoon dark rum
1 teaspoon vanilla
6 eggs, at room
  temperature
1/2 cup sugar
1 cup heavy cream,
  whipped
Extra whipped cream
  on the side

DESSERTS

Mississippi Mud Cake

Marshmallows have not always been fluffy: they were originally a hard candy made from the sweetened extract of the roots and leaves of the marshmallow plant. A folk remedy for sore throats is a tea made from the peeled and boiled marshmallow root mixed with honey. Nowadays this typically American treat is made mostly of sugar—just perfect to top off this decadent cake.

SERVES 12 or more

Cake:
Butter and flour for the cake pan
1 cup butter
2 cups sugar
4 eggs
1-1/2 cup flour
1/3 cup cocoa
1 cup coarsely chopped pecans
1 teaspoon vanilla
3 cups miniature marshmallows

To make the cake:
Preheat the oven to 350°.

Butter both the bottom and sides of a 9x13-inch pan. Add a little flour and shake it around to coat the bottom and sides of the pan. Shake out the excess.

In a large bowl, combine the butter and sugar. Beat well until creamy. Add the eggs, one at a time, beating thoroughly after each addition.

In a separate bowl, sift together the flour and the cocoa. Fold this into the creamed mixture. Add the pecans and vanilla and beat well.

Spoon the cake mixture into the prepared pan and smooth it over. Bake at 350° for 30 to 35 minutes. Remove from the oven and sprinkle the top with the miniature marshmallows. Return to the oven and bake for about 10 minutes more until the marshmallows melt and are starting to brown. Remove from the oven and let cool in the pan for 30 minutes.

BEST RECIPES OF BERKSHIRE CHEFS

To make the icing:
In a saucepan, melt the butter.

Sift together the confectioners' sugar and the cocoa. Stir into the melted butter along with the pecans and evaporated milk.

Spread the icing over the cake and let stand until thoroughly cooled.

Icing:
1 cup butter
1 pound confectioners' sugar
1/3 cup cocoa
1 cup coarsely chopped pecans
1/2 cup evaporated milk

Chocolate Almond Cake

For an attractive variation, cover the top of this cake with slivered almonds.
This delicious dessert freezes well, too.

SERVES 6 to 8

Cake:

4 ounces semisweet chocolate

2 tablespoons rum

1/2 cup butter, softened

2/3 cup granulated sugar

3 egg yolks

3 egg whites

Pinch of salt

1 tablespoon sugar

1/3 cup pulverized almonds

1/4 teaspoon almond extract

3/4 cup cake flour, sifted twice

To make the cake:

Preheat the oven to 350°.

Butter and flour an 8-inch round cake pan. Melt the chocolate in the top of a double boiler over simmering water. Stir in the rum.

Cream the butter and sugar until fluffy and pale yellow. Add the egg yolks and beat until well blended.

In a separate bowl, beat the egg whites until stiff peaks are formed.

Blend the chocolate into the butter mixture. Stir in the almonds and almond extract. Sir in one quarter of the egg whites and one quarter of the flour, and blend gently. Repeat until all is blended.

Pour the batter into the prepared pan, pushing the batter up to the rim with a spatula. Bake in the middle of the oven at 350° for about 25 minutes until the cake is puffed but the center still moves slightly when you shake the pan.

Allow the cake to cool for about 10 minutes and then turn it out onto a cake rack. Cool for 1 to 2 hours before spreading on the icing.

BEST RECIPES OF BERKSHIRE CHEFS

To make the icing:

Stir the chocolate and rum in the top of a double boiler over simmering water until melted into a smooth cream.

Remove from the heat and beat in the butter, a tablespoon at a time, until smooth.

Place the pan over cold water and whip until the icing stiffens to spreading consistency. Spread quickly over the cooled cake. Garnish with slivered almonds if desired.

Icing:
1 ounce semisweet chocolate
1 tablespoon rum
3 tablespoons unsalted butter

Slivered almonds for garnish (optional)

Shaker Chocolate Pound Cake

HANCOCK SHAKER VILLAGE

When staff members at the Hancock Shaker Village demonstrate Shaker cooking in the 1830 kitchen with this recipe, the fragrance of chocolate draws visitors from throughout the village looking for a sample.

MAKES one tube cake

Butter and flour for the pan
1 cup butter
1/2 cup lard
3 cups sugar
5 eggs
3 cups sifted flour
1/2 cup sifted cocoa
1/2 teaspoon baking powder
1/4 teaspoon salt
1-1/4 cup milk
2 tablespoons grated chocolate
1 teaspoon vanilla
Whipped cream (optional)
Shaved chocolate (optional)

Preheat the oven to 325°.

Butter and flour a tube pan.

In a large mixing bowl, cream the butter, lard, and sugar together until they are light and fluffy. Add the eggs, one at a time, beating well after each addition.

Sift together the flour, cocoa, baking powder, and salt. Add these dry ingredients alternately with the milk to the egg mixture, stirring after each addition until well blended.

Add the grated chocolate. Stir in the vanilla.

Turn the batter into the prepared pan. Bake at 325° for 1-1/2 hour.

Turn out onto a wire rack to cool. Fill the center with whipped cream and sprinkle with shaved chocolate if desired.

Almond Torte

THE EGREMONT INN

Native to India, the almond tree was brought to the Arab world. The Arabs in their turn introduced the almond to Europe, and from there it made its way to the New World. In the Berkshires, the well-traveled almond happily comes to rest on this torte.

Preheat the oven to 325°.

To make the crust:
Combine the flour and sugar in the bowl of a food processor. And the butter pieces and process until the mixture has the texture of corn meal. Add the egg yolks and process until combined.

Press the dough into a springform pan, pushing a rim up the sides about 1 inch high. Bake for 10 minutes at 325°.

Remove the crust and set the oven to 375°.

To make the filling:
In a saucepan, stir together the cream, sugar, and salt. Bring to a boil over medium heat, stirring frequently. Simmer for 5 minutes, stirring occasionally. Add the almonds and almond extract.

Pour into the crust and bake at 375° for 30 minutes or until lightly browned on top.

SERVES 9 to 12

Crust:
1 cup flour
1-1/2 tablespoon sugar
6 tablespoons unsalted butter, in pieces
2 egg yolks

Filling:
1 cup heavy cream
1 cup sugar
1/4 teaspoon salt
1 cup sliced almonds
1/4 teaspoon almond extract

Lemon Yogurt Cake

ELEANOR TILLINGHAST

"I love desserts, but try to avoid the customary fat. So, working from an old Turkish recipe, I came up with this lusciously light cake. Although it tastes rich, the only added fat is in the eggs, which amounts to less than 2 grams per serving. Since this recipe contains so very little fat, its preparation, although easy, is quite precise. Follow these simple steps exactly and you'll create a really special dessert."

SERVES 12

8 ounces nonfat plain yogurt (without gelatin, gums, or other stabilizers)
4 extra large eggs
Parchment paper for the pan
2/3 cup all-purpose flour
1/4 cup cornstarch
1/4 cup plus 3/4 cup plus 2 tablespoons superfine sugar

Spoon the yogurt into a yogurt strainer or a sieve lined with a triple layer of damp cheesecloth. Place over a large bowl, cover, and refrigerate for 8 hours to yield 1/2 cup yogurt cheese. Discard the whey.

Separate the eggs, placing the whites into one large mixing bowl and the yolks into another.

Line the bottom of a 12-cup capacity tube pan with parchment paper.

Preheat the oven to 325° if using a non-stick, dark, or glass pan, or to 350° for a light or shiny pan. Adjust the oven rack to the center position.

Sift and then measure the flour. Sift and then measure the cornstarch.

Sift together the flour, cornstarch, and the 1/4 cup sugar.

Using an electric mixer at high speed, beat the egg yolks for 10 minutes, adding the 3/4 cup sugar in a slow stream during the last few minutes.

Using a fork, mix the yogurt cheese, baking soda, and lemon oil for a minute. The mixture will foam and expand.

With the electric mixer at low speed, quickly blend the yogurt mixture into the egg yolks.

Using clean beaters, whip the egg whites until foamy. Add the cream of tartar. Continue whipping until soft peaks form. Add the 2 tablespoons sugar in a slow stream and beat until stiff but not dry. Avoid overbeating.

Stir a cupful of the egg whites into the yogurt mixture. Spoon the remaining whites on top of the mixture and sift the flour mixture over them. Gently fold in, incorporating thoroughly so the baked cake won't look streaked.

Distribute the batter evenly in the pan, being careful not to deflate the beaten egg whites. Draw a spatula through the batter to eliminate air bubbles.

Bake for 35 minutes or until the cake feels spongy to the touch. Do not open the oven door during the first 20 minutes.

Remove the cake from the oven and immediately invert onto a long-necked bottle, as for angel food cake, and let cool completely before removing.

Serve the cake plain or ice it with your favorite lowfat lemon frosting.

1 teaspoon baking soda
1-1/2 teaspoons
    pure lemon oil (or
    3 tablespoons grated
    lemon rind *plus* 1
    teaspoon pure lemon
    extract)
1/2 teaspoon cream of
    tartar

Mumu's Apple Cake

SELMA JACOBS VAN PRAAGH

*This book is dedicated to my Mom for many reasons,
only one of which is that she is a fine cook. Since she is Dutch, it makes sense
that an apple cake figures in her repertory. She has been making this cake for as long
as I can remember and has delighted family and guests with it on four continents.*

SERVES 9

Butter and flour for the
   pan
2 apples
3/4 cup sugar
1/4 cup softened
   margarine
1 egg
1/2 cup milk
1-1/2 cup flour
2 teaspoons baking
   powder
2 tablespoons sugar
1 teaspoon cinnamon

Preheat the oven to 375°.

Butter and flour a 9-inch square pan.

Cut the unpeeled apples into quarters' core and cut the sections into three slices each. Set aside.

In a bowl combine the 3/4 cup sugar, margarine, and egg. With an electric beater, mix thoroughly. Stir in the milk.

In a separate bowl, sift together the flour and baking powder. Stir the flour into the creamed sugar mixture until thoroughly mixed.

Spread the batter into the prepared pan. Arrange the apple slices in three rows on top of the batter. Push the slices slightly into the batter, using this motion to spread the batter to the edges of the pan. Mix the 2 tablespoons sugar with the cinnamon and sprinkle on top.

Bake at 375° for 25 to 35 minutes or until a wooden skewer inserted in the middle of the pan comes out clean.

This recipe can easily be (and usually is) doubled.

BEST RECIPES OF BERKSHIRE CHEFS

Grandma Horka's Plum Cake

TAFT FARMS

*Says Taft granddaughter Martha, "The food flavors and aromas experienced
in childhood evoke memories which can never be extinguished. So it is with this cake:
I have vivid memories of Grandma Horka making this confection using
the prune plums that grew on the tree behind our house. It seemed as though she always
had some on hand to serve to my brothers and me when we came to visit.
This is a simple but cherished recipe in our family."*

Preheat the oven to 350°.

Butter one 9x12-inch pan or two 9-inch round pans. Sift together the flour, baking powder, and salt. Set aside.

In a separate bowl, beat the egg slightly. Add the sugar, oil, and milk, and mix with the egg.

Add the egg mixture to the flour mixture and stir until combined. Spread thinly into the prepared pan or pans. Arrange a layer of plum halves on the batter until the batter is completely covered.

For the glaze:
Combine the ingredients and spread over the plums.

Bake at 350° for 30 minutes.

SERVES 12

Butter for the cake pan
2 cups flour
3 teaspoons double-acting baking powder
1 teaspoon salt
1 egg
3 tablespoons sugar
2 tablespoons canola oil
3/4 cup milk
1 pint (about 24) fresh prune plums, halved and pitted (enough to cover the batter in a single layer)

Glaze:
1 egg
1/2 cup sugar
2 tablespoons milk

Pumpkin Chocolate Cheesecake

ALICE BROCK

Alice gave this recipe to Arlo Guthrie.
It's a particular favorite with the Guthrie Center staff.

MAKES *one 9-inch cake*

Crust:
Butter for the pan
1-1/2 cup graham
   cracker or gingersnap
   crumbs
1/2 cup melted butter
1 cup brown sugar

Filling:
16 ounces cream cheese,
   softened
1/2 cup heavy cream
4 eggs
1/4 cup brown sugar
1 cup canned, or
   cooked and puréed,
   pumpkin
4 ounces Bakers
   German Sweet
   Chocolate
1/4 to 1/2 teaspoon
   each ground cloves,
   ground cinnamon,
   and ground ginger

Preheat the oven to 350°.

Place a pan of water on the bottom shelf of the oven. Butter a 9-inch springform pan.

To make the crust:
Combine the ingredients and press into the bottom of the buttered springform pan.

To make the filling:
With an electric beater, whip together the cream cheese and 1/4 cup of the heavy cream. Add the eggs, brown sugar, pumpkin, and spices and mix until smooth.

In a double boiler, melt the chocolate. Stir in the remaining 1/4 cup heavy cream. Swirl the chocolate mixture into the pumpkin mixture. Don't overmix.

Pour into the prepared crust and bake at 350° for 1 hour on the top shelf of the oven.

Let the cheesecake cool at room temperature, and chill overnight if you can wait.

BEST RECIPES OF BERKSHIRE CHEFS

Lime Cheesecake

THE WILLIAMSVILLE INN

"The most luscious, creamy cheesecake you've ever had! Yes, it's totally fattening. But some things you've just got to do," says chef Stephen Daoust.

Preheat the oven to 300°.

Mix the crushed chocolate wafers with the melted butter and press the mixture into the bottom and 1 inch up the sides of a 9-inch springform pan. Chill.

Mix the eggs and the 1 cup sugar with a blender for several minutes until pale yellow. Add the lime juice and vanilla and combine.

In a bowl, cream the cream cheese until soft, and slowly add the egg-and-sugar mixture. Fill the prepared pan and bake at 300° for 50 minutes or until the top is set. Allow to cool.

In a separate bowl, mix the sour cream with the 1/4 cup sugar and spoon over the top of the cooled cake. Bake for 10 minutes more. Chill overnight.

Run a sharp, thin knife between the crust and the pan before you unmold the cake.

SERVES 8

9-ounce package chocolate wafers, finely crushed
4 tablespoons butter, melted
3 extra large eggs
1 cup sugar
1/2 cup fresh lime juice
1 tablespoon vanilla
24 ounces cream cheese
16 ounces sour cream
1/4 cup sugar

Chocolate Caramel Pie

20 RAILROAD STREET

*The pride of 20 Railroad Street is the 28-foot-long mahogany bar,
moved from its old home at the Commodore Hotel in New York City
to Great Barrington in 1919. During the Prohibition era, the establishment became
a speakeasy; it did obtain an official liquor license in 1933. Railroad Street now offers
a varied menu, from snacks to full meals, and at the bar it makes good on its promise
to provide spirits and conversation.*

SERVES 8 to 10

Crust:
1-3/4 cup ground
   almonds
1/3 cup granulated
   sugar
1/4 cup melted butter

Filling:
1-1/2 cup cream
12 ounces semisweet
   chocolate, chopped

Topping sauce:
1/2 cup butter
1 cup sugar
1 cup heavy cream

Preheat the oven to 375°.

To make the crust:
In a bowl, mix the ingredients. Press the mixture into a 10-inch pie plate and bake at 375°. When the pie comes out of the oven, the shell will have puffed up a little. Push it down with a fork to flatten it.

To make the filling:
In a heavy saucepan, heat the cream to boiling. Add the chocolate and stir until all the chocolate is melted and the mixture is smooth. Pour into the pie shell and let it chill and set in the refrigerator.

To make the topping sauce:
In a heavy saucepan, melt the butter with the sugar until the sugar is golden brown. Add the heavy cream and stir until smooth. Be careful because the mixture might foam up when you add the cream.

Spoon warm sauce over each slice of pie.

BEST RECIPES OF BERKSHIRE CHEFS

Butterscotch Schnapps Pie

THE SPRINGS RESTAURANT

The Springs achieves an effect of comfort and warmth rare in contemporary interiors, and to this it adds a well-deserved reputation for fine and reliable cuisine— it was one of the earliest recipients of the Mobil four-star designation in Massachusetts. This combination, along with a location convenient to both Williamstown and Pittsfield, has made it a popular retreat for residents and visitors in beautiful North County.

Preheat the oven to 350°.

To make the crust:
Cut the shortening into the flour until the shortening is the size of walnuts.

Add the salt and the sugar and then the cold water. Mix only until just combined: do not overmix. Roll out on a floured surface and put into a 9-inch pie plate.

To make the filling:
Place the ingredients into a bowl and mix very well. Pour into the prepared pie crust.

Bake at 350° for 45 to 60 minutes. You can tell that the pie is done when it wiggles like a jelled dessert.

During the last 5 minutes of baking, sprinkle the crushed Butterscotch Disks over the top of the pie.

Serve cold. Drizzle some butterscotch schnapps over each slice of pie and top with whipped cream.

SERVES 8

Crust:
1-1/2 cup flour
1 cup shortening
1/2 cup cold water
Pinch of salt
Pinch of sugar

Filling:
9 eggs
3/4 cup sugar
1/2 cup butterscotch
 schnapps
3 cups half-and-half
Pinch of nutmeg

Topping:
3-ounce package of
 Brach's Butterscotch
 Disks, crushed very
 fine
Butterscotch schnapps
 for garnish
Whipped cream for
 garnish

Cranberry Walnut Tart

SUCHÈLE BAKERS

*Tucked into a side street in Lenox, this bakery creates superb breads and pastries.
Says owner Susan Berzinis, "We use only fresh ingredients and make all items
from scratch. We try to make the most of any fresh fruit in season.
We use a lot of cranberries in the fall, in muffins, pies, cakes, and Danish fillings."*

SERVES 8

Tart shell:
2-1/2 cups flour
3 tablespoons sugar
1 cup cold unsalted
    butter, in pieces
4 teaspoons ice water
2 egg yolks

To make the tart shell:
Preheat the oven to 400°.

Place the flour and sugar into the bowl of a food processor. Add the pieces of butter and process for 10 seconds until the mixture resembles coarse meal.

Whisk together the ice water and egg yolks. While the processor is running, add the yolk mixture slowly through the feed tube until the dough holds together.

Take the dough out and pat it into a flat ball. Wrap it in plastic wrap and chill it in the refrigerator for at least 1 hour.

Roll the dough out on a lightly floured surface to 1/8 inch thick. Press into a 9-inch tart pan with a removable rim, turning under the 1-inch overhang to reinforce the edge. Chill for 1 hour.

Lightly prick the shell with a fork. Line the uncooked shell with aluminum foil, pressing into the edges. Weight the foil down with pie weights or dried beans (you can reserve beans for this purpose and reuse them).

BEST RECIPES OF BERKSHIRE CHEFS

Bake for 15 to 18 minutes at 400°. When the pastry begins to color, remove the foil and beans: the pastry is now partially cooked for the cranberry walnut tart. (If you want to use the shell for a recipe which requires a fully baked shell, continue baking after you remove the aluminum foil and the beans until the pastry dries out and turns a light golden color.)

To make the filling:
Preheat the oven to 350°.

Whisk together the eggs, brown sugar, and corn syrup. Add the butter, salt, and vanilla. Stir in the cranberries and walnuts.

Pour the cranberry walnut filling into the prebaked tart shell. Bake at 350° for 25 to 30 minutes or until set.

Filling:
3 eggs
2/3 cup brown sugar
2/3 cup light corn syrup
1/4 cup unsalted butter, melted and cooled
1/2 teaspoon salt
1 teaspoon vanilla
1-1/4 cup coarsely chopped cranberries
1 cup chopped walnuts

Apple Cranberry Pie

THE OLD INN ON THE GREEN

The extra lemon juice and zest give this pie a tartness which distinguishes it from the rest. A perfect ending to a Thanksgiving dinner—and a delicious choice throughout the winter, with cranberries from the freezer.

MAKES one 9-inch pie

Pie crust dough for a
9-inch two-crust pie
8 large, tart apples
(Granny Smiths or
Macouns are ideal)
Juice and zest of 1/2
lemon
2-1/2 cups sugar
1-1/2 teaspoon
cinnamon
2 cups cranberries
3 tablespoons flour
Egg wash, made from 1
egg yolk mixed with
1 tablespoon water
Sugar

Preheat the oven to 375°.

Line a 9-inch glass pie plate with pie crust dough. Trim the dough so that it is even with the pie plate edge.

Peel, core, and quarter the apples. Cut each quarter into 1-inch chunks. Put these into a large bowl and sprinkle them with the lemon juice and zest, sugar, and cinnamon. Mix well.

Add the cranberries and flour. Mix again, taking care not to cut into the apples.

Spoon the mixture into the pie shell. Top with either a lattice or a solid top crust. Crimp the edges together. Slash the top if a solid top crust is used. Brush with the egg wash and sprinkle lightly with sugar.

Bake at 375° for 45 minutes or until the crust is golden brown and the juices running out of the pie are thickened.

Lemon Chèvre Pie

RAWSON BROOK FARM

*On a back road in Monterey is a lovely farm with goats in all sizes and colors.
You can easily get to know them since they all wear big name tags. The wonderful
cheese made from their milk is available in a variety of flavors at Rawson Brook Farm
as well as in most local stores, and its subtle taste enhances many dishes.*

Combine the 1 cup sugar and the cornstarch. Stir in the water, lemon peel, lemon juice, and egg yolks. Cook in a double boiler, stirring constantly until thickened.

Remove from the heat and add the Monterey Chèvre. Cool.

In a separate bowl, beat the egg whites. When they start to form soft peaks, add the 1/4 cup sugar. Whip until the mixture is stiff.

Fold the egg whites into the lemon mixture. Pour into the pie shell and chill well.

SERVES 8

1 cup sugar
1/4 cup cornstarch
1 cup water
1 teaspoon grated
  lemon peel
1/3 cup lemon juice
2 egg yolks, beaten
4 ounces unsalted or
  plain Monterey
  Chèvre
2 egg whites
1/4 cup sugar
8-inch pie shell, baked
  and cooled

Lemon Pie

SADIE'S PIES

"My grandmother Sarah Nash Waltman, who lived in Louisville, Kentucky, was a fabulous cook and we would always look forward to her Sunday suppers. My favorite was fried chicken and mashed potatoes with cream gravy and she would finish off with this lemon pie. When I was learning to bake she told me that the secret to this pie is cooking the filling for a full 8 minutes before adding the egg yolks. The long cooking gives the filling a wonderful silk-like quality that is missing in most meringue pies." Sarah Burke, the owner of Sadie's Pies, was the pie maker for Miss Ruby's Café. Its famous pies are still available courtesy of Sarah's catering.

SERVES 8

Lemon filling;
1-1/2 cup sugar
3 tablespoons
    cornstarch
3 tablespoons flour
Dash of salt
2-1/2 cups hot water
3 egg yolks, lightly
    beaten
3 tablespoons butter
1/2 teaspoon grated
    lemon peel
1/3 cup lemon juice

10-inch pie shell, baked
    and cooled

To make the lemon filling:
In a medium, nonaluminum saucepan, sift together the sugar, cornstarch, flour, and salt. Gradually add the hot water, stirring constantly with a wire whisk.

Bring the mixture to a quick boil, stirring all the while. Reduce the heat and continue to cook the mixture for a full 8 minutes, stirring constantly.

Meanwhile, beat the egg yolks in a small bowl. Pour a bit of the hot mixture into the eggs, stirring constantly to warm the eggs and keep them from curdling when added to the hot mixture. Quickly stir the egg mixture back into the pan and bring to a boil again. Reduce the heat and cook for 4 more minutes.

Remove from the heat and add the butter and lemon peel. Stir until the butter is melted. Gradually stir in the lemon juice.

Pour into the baked pie shell and cool to room temperature.

BEST RECIPES OF BERKSHIRE CHEFS

To make the meringue:
Preheat the oven to 350°.

While the filling is cooling, prepare the meringue by beating the egg whites into soft peaks. Then gradually add, one teaspoon at a time, the lemon juice and sugar. Continue beating until the meringue forms stiff peaks.

Spoon the meringue over the cooled filling, making sure you seal it to the edges.

Bake the pie at 350° for 12 to 15 minutes or until the meringue is nicely browned.

Meringue:
3 egg whites
1 teaspoon lemon juice
6 tablespoons sugar

Chef's Blueberry Pie

THE RED LION INN

*Chef Steven Douglas Mongeon has been executive chef of the Red Lion Inn
for more than a decade. A graduate of the Culinary Institute of America, he is
a culinary instructor at Berkshire Community College. He is also a member of
the Berkshire County Chapter of the American Culinary Federation, where he has twice
served as vice president. He has received numerous professional and culinary awards.*

YIELDS one 10-inch pie

Crust:
1/4 cup cold butter
1/4 cup shortening
1 cup plus 1 tablespoon
    flour
1/2 teaspoon salt
1/4 cup cold milk

To make the crust:
In a small bowl, blend the butter and
shortening together with a wooden
spoon.

In a large bowl, sift the flour and salt
together. Cut in the butter-shortening
mixture, using a pastry blender or two
knives, until the mixture resembles
cornmeal.

Add the cold milk, and blend until it is
absorbed.

(If using a food processor, place the
butter, shortening, flour, and salt into
the bowl; fit with a steel blade. Process
until the mixture resembles cornmeal.
With the processor on, add the milk
slowly through the funnel until the
dough forms a ball.)

Roll the dough into a ball, wrap it in
plastic wrap, and refrigerate until
chilled, about 30 minutes.

To make the filling:
In a large bowl, toss together the blueberries, flour, and the 1 cup sugar.

Add the Grand Marnier and mix.

To complete the pie:
Preheat the oven to 450°.

Roll out half of the dough and line a 10-inch pie plate. Spoon the filling into the crust. Roll out the other half of the dough, place over the filling, and crimp the edges together.

Brush the top with the 1 tablespoon milk and sprinkle with the sugar.

Bake at 450° degrees for 10 minutes. Turn the oven down to 350° and bake for 35 to 40 minutes more, until golden brown.

Serve warm with ice cream.

Filling:
3 pints fresh blueberries, picked over
1/4 cup flour
1 cup sugar
1 tablespoon Grand Marnier

1 tablespoon milk
1 tablespoon sugar

Chess Pie

DRAGON BREADS

The breads, pies, and other treats prepared by Mary Alcantara are available at many outlets in the Berkshires. Her distinctive Dragon Breads logo is a guarantee of a delicious homemade creation.

SERVES 6 to 8

Crust:
1/4 cup butter
1 tablespoons vegetable shortening
1 cup flour
2 tablespoons sugar
Ice water as needed

Filling:
1/2 cup butter
3 tablespoons sugar
3 eggs
1-1/2 cup table syrup
2 teaspoons vanilla
1 cup coarsely chopped pecans
1/2 cup raisins

Preheat the oven to 350°.

To make the crust:
With an electric mixer, combine the butter, shortening, flour, and sugar until it has a sandy consistency. Add the ice water, a teaspoon at a time, until the mixture holds together.

Roll out the dough and line a pie plate with it. Crimp the edges.

To make the filling:
In the large bowl of an electric mixer, cream the butter until fluffy. Add the sugar and mix well. Then add the eggs, one at a time, and beat well. Add the table syrup and vanilla and mix well. Finally, add the pecans and raisins and mix.

Pour the filling into the prepared pie crust and bake at 350° for 30 minutes. The filling will not be completely set. Allow the pie to cool before cutting it.

White-Chocolate Pumpkin Chimichangas

ENCORE! ENCORE!

This recipe is one of the restaurant's signature desserts:
tortillas and style from the Southwest, cranberries and pumpkin from the Berkshires.
This daring and unusual mix of flavors is a spectacular finish
for a dinner party!

To make the filling:
Mix the sugar and cinnamon. Reserve half and set aside.

Place the remaining cinnamon-sugar mixture into bowl. Stir in the pumpkin, white chocolate chips, and cranberries.

In separate bowl, whip the cream. Fold into the pumpkin mixture.

To prepare the tortillas:
Spoon one quarter of the filling across the center of each tortilla in a 1-inch band. Roll up the tortilla tightly. Sauté in the butter until evenly and lightly browned and roll immediately in the reserved cinnamon-sugar.

Microwave on high for 30 seconds.

To make the fruit salsa:
Mix the fruit salsa ingredients.

Serve over the chimichangas.

SERVES 4

Filling:
2 cups sugar
1/2 teaspoon cinnamon
1/2 can (one-pie size) canned pumpkin
1/4 cup white chocolate chips
1/4 cup chopped cranberries
1 cup whipping cream

Tortillas:
4 flour tortillas, 8" or 9"
1/4 cup melted butter

Fruit salsa:
1/4 cup finely diced cantaloupe
1/4 cup finely diced honeydew
1/4 cup finely diced pineapple
1/4 cup finely diced strawberries

Hot Blueberries with Vanilla Ice Cream

THE ELM COURT INN

This is a delightful and unusual dessert to make after picking your own blueberries—Blueberry Hill Farm in Mount Washington is a favorite place.

SERVES 4

2 oranges
1 lemon
1 lime
1/2 cup sugar
1/4 cup water
2 tablespoons butter
1/4 cup Grand Marnier
2 tablespoons kirsch
1 pint blueberries
   (reserve some for
   garnish)
4 scoops of vanilla ice
   cream
Mint leaves for garnish

Remove the zest from the citrus fruits and set aside. Juice all the citrus and set that aside.

Pour the sugar and water into a heavy saucepan and stir with a wooden spoon until the sugar caramelizes to a light brown. Add the citrus juices, being very careful not to splatter, and the zest. The caramel will suddenly harden, but keep stirring over medium heat until it dissolves completely.

Add the butter, Grand Marnier, and kirsch. (The sauce can also be made without the liqueurs, if desired.) Bring to a boil carefully (on a gas stove, you will set fire to the mixture if the flame is too high).

Add the blueberries, remove from the heat, and let stand for 2 minutes.

Serve in bowls with one scoop of vanilla ice cream for each serving. Garnish with mint leaves.

Index

The line art for the cover and text
was drawn by Elizabeth Barbour,
freelance illustrator and painter.

Type was set in Palatino on
PageMaker by Rodelinde Albrecht,
freelance designer and editor.